✋ The Glory Series ✋

It is not necessary to have read *Living for His Glory*, the first book in The Glory Series, to enjoy and glean insights from Reflecting His Glory. Although part of a series, this book stands on its own, inviting readers along on a journey to uncover nuggets of inspiration for living a purposeful and impactful life. A life glorifying God.

- ### *Living for His Glory* (Book #1)

Explore the essence of a life devoted to God. Seeking the glory of God in the ordinary rhythms of life and amidst sudden, jarring challenges is not our default. It requires intentional effort to avoid doing what is merely convenient, comfortable, and easy. As we live by faith for the glory of God, we find the deep-seated peace and joy we crave—the abundant life! This is a life of profound significance that will echo with eternal impact.

- ### *Reflecting His Glory* (Book #2)

Discover the life-changing journey of transformation that unfolds when we intentionally pursue His glory in the rhythms of our everyday life. As we do, His glory fills us to overflowing. Unable to be contained, it is set ablaze from within. His glory bursts forth, shining in and beyond us in visible, tangible ways. It's radical! We become a blinding reflection of His glory, piercing and shattering the darkness all around us as the extraordinary transects the ordinary. People are drawn to this radiant light, and we become a beacon of hope in a desperate world, impacting not just our immediate circles of family and friends but those well beyond.

- ### *Rejoicing in His Glory* (Book #3)

Step into the deep, lasting joy that comes when we fully embrace living for the magnificent glory of God. As we reflect the brilliance of Christ into a dark and weary world—unshaken by cultural values or the temptation to compromise—His glory becomes our steady anchor. And in that sacred place of surrender, we discover our greatest sustaining joy. A joy that holds. A joy that transforms. A joy that shines.

Praise for *Reflecting His Glory*

"This inspiring work offers a profound journey toward a life of purpose and significance. Filled with wisdom and inspiration, Kinney guides readers to persevere through suffering, discover renewed purpose, and live a life that makes an impact for eternity. Each well-organized chapter is a testament to the power of faith and the transformative impact of reflecting God's glory in our lives. Kinney offers a confident and caring narrative that makes readers feel as though they're in safe hands, offering inspiring and kind words that resonate long after the book is finished. The book serves as a beacon of hope in a desperate world. Reflecting His Glory is a must-read for anyone seeking spiritual growth, a deeper connection with their faith, and a deeply enriching experience that will leave them feeling uplifted and transformed."

READERS' FAVORITE 5-star Review

"This book will challenge and inspire you! Whether you're exploring the faith or a lifelong Christ-follower, you'll uncover spiritual gems that reveal the profound impact you have on those around you. Kim's skillful blend of biblical wisdom, delightful humor, and encouraging words not only will engage you, but will also motivate you to keep pushing through life's trials - because those around you need it!"

David Benham
Best-Selling Author, Entrepreneur

"Kim has the winsome ability to laugh at herself while teaching spiritual truth. With a goal of reflecting the Savior's glory, Kim's stories capture the heart while directing the spirit to yield to His transforming grace. With the yielding comes the desire and ability to mirror the awesomeness of God to other longing souls so they, too, can experience His grace."

Tricia Scribner, PhD
Author of *LifeGivers Apologetics*

"Kim has done it again! A fitting sequel to Living for His Glory, this book is both edifying and engrossing. Every page is rich in Scripture and adorned with anecdotes that I trust the Lord will use to shatter the darkness for all who read, that they might shine the light of Christ through life's joys and sorrows."

Kyler Smith, PhD
Senior Associate Pastor
Hickory Grove Baptist Church in Charlotte, NC

"Who among us truly understands what it means that 'God created us for His glory?' Such a complex topic; and yet Kim gently and artfully walks with us in illuminating the answer. Armed with Scripture, Kim makes the abstract accessible by building on our concrete and universal experiences that unequivocally echo His Word. This book is a must read for believers and nonbelievers alike."

Representative Kristin Baker, MD
NC State House

"As someone who has had the privilege of delving into the profound insights shared by Kim Kinney in her previous work, "Living for His Glory," I am thrilled to endorse her latest masterpiece. With each page, Kim leads us closer to the radiant splendor of God's majesty, inviting us to marvel at His infinite wisdom, unfathomable love, and boundless grace. Whether you are a seasoned theologian, a seeker of spiritual truths, or simply a soul longing for a deeper encounter with the divine, this book offers invaluable insights and profound revelations that will enrich your journey and deepen your relationship with God."

Hannah Arrowood
Founder and Executive Director
Present Age Ministries

REFLECTING
HIS
Glory

SHATTER THE DARKNESS
AS YOU SHINE
THE *Light of Christ* THROUGH
LIFE'S JOYS AND SORROWS

Kim S. Kinney

Paperback ISBN: 978-1-958770-03-0
eBook ISBN: 978-1-958770-02-3
Large Print ISBN: 978-1-958770-04-7
Hardcover ISBN: 978-1-958770-05-4

Cover Art by Cinque, 99designs.

www.kimskinney.com

⸺❈⸺

Other Bible Translations Used

Cover Inspiration

In the Old Testament, God's presence and glory were often veiled by a thick cloud, shielding His holiness from the sight of His people, as it was deemed too sacred for human eyes. Yet His glory is always shining, piercing the darkness of the world as it reflects the majesty of God. While God remains physically unseen, He graciously reveals His splendor through nature.

This cover design captures the magnificence of God's glory, hidden from our eyes, yet bursting forth with brilliance in nature. As we gaze at the heavens, the rugged mountain peaks, and the vast diversity of plant and animal life, we witness His glory shining through, reflecting His holiness. Contemplating the enormity of God's greatness takes our breath away in awe and wonder. We can hardly take it in.

Disclaimer

In retelling Scripture, I have allowed myself the freedom to expand upon the stories by imagining details, personal thoughts, and emotions of the characters. These additions are not meant to alter the biblical narrative but to bring the stories to life in an engaging and thought-provoking way, while remaining faithful to the heart of the message.

Author's Note

For purposes of clarity and respect, I have taken the liberty of capitalizing all pronouns referring to the divinity, except for direct quotations from Scripture.

Dedication

I lovingly dedicate my second book to my parents, Arthur and Marian Schumacher, who both made a significant imprint on my life. They raised me and my brother, Scott, in a loving home filled with support and encouragement.

Most importantly, they raised us in a God-fearing home. We were in church every Sunday, went to Sunday School, and attended Vacation Bible School in the summers. I also attended confirmation classes every Saturday morning for two years, minus the summers. I never complained as I grew to cherish this time with our pastor who made learning and memorization fun.

We changed churches when I was 14. At a pivotal age, I didn't fit in with the cliques long since established. I begged to be allowed to skip Sunday School, but quickly learned this was not an option. My parents essentially told me, "You need to be in Sunday School. We're sorry your feelings are hurt. Figure something out." The message was clear: Sunday School and church were non-negotiable. I wouldn't be allowed to skip this essential spiritual discipline.

I decided to leave the torment and pettiness of the high school girls' drama behind. So, at age 15, I offered to teach Sunday School. The church staff reluctantly gave me a second-grade class of twenty boys—a class every teacher avoided. Young and naïve, I agreed to teach—and did so for two years with a friend, also my age. I loved it!

Looking back, I am thankful my parents held strong and kept me in church. It made all the difference.

I also dedicate this book to my husband and children. Bob, Justin, and Rebecca, God knew I would need each of you in unique and special ways throughout my life. And I treasure you—fiercely.

You loved me through all the writing and research. You encouraged me through the editing, which again proved most painful. I can't thank you enough for being the critical eyes to read through the unfinished manuscript and offer your input which I greatly cherish.

Justin, as an author yourself, you have been a tremendous help with all the moving parts, mind-numbing details, and the profound frustration associated with the process of publishing a book. This book wouldn't be here without you.

I sincerely thank each of you for your unwavering and loving devotion. You are dearly loved and appreciated.

Connect with me

I am delighted you have chosen to read *Reflecting His Glory*, the second book in The Glory Series.

Please visit my website and get a free gift, which will be emailed to you. See the image on page 299.

kimskinney.com

Follow me on Facebook and Instagram:
@KimSKinneyauthor

Amazon author page:
amazon.com/author/kimskinney

Or email me:
Kim@kimskinney.com

Welcome

You could have chosen any book on the shelf, yet you chose this one. Maybe you were drawn to the title or the cover design. Perhaps you read the first book in The Glory Series, *Living for His Glory*, and sought out the second book. Regardless, I believe you were led here for a reason. Possibly for yourself or for a loved one. I pray you find what your spirit is craving… the power of God behind the words I've penned.

God's glory: it's all around us, yet we can't even begin to fathom it. If I were to write this book based on my own insight and knowledge, you'd be staring at blank pages. But God… He has been gracious to allow me a small role as He reveals what it means to live life reflecting His glory.

Each chapter stands on its own merit. The writing style and topics vary. Some are historical, others more contemporary. Some are in-depth biblical insights, others a lighter read. Yet they're all intricately woven together in a delicate balance—much like a tapestry lovingly crafted, each thread reflecting the splendor of the grand design. Make use of the topical index in the back. Note that Scripture references are cited at the end of each chapter and bibliographical references are listed at the end of the book.

Explore divine truths tucked within the folds of these pages as we consider what it means to reflect His glory. May He guide your reading. And may He lovingly bless you in abundance for the precious time you spend reflecting on His majesty. Let's begin together.

Kim S. Kinney

Contents

Contents

Introduction

"We are all starved for the glory of God."[A]
John Piper

God created us in His glory, for His glory, to reflect His glory. Easy to say, beautiful to read, but what does this really mean?

Imagine a large prism with numerous flat, polished, crystal faces reflecting light. All the intricately cut faces surround the center at slightly different and distinct angles, each one a tiny aspect of the whole. Alone, each crystal face, while beautiful, reflects only a small part. But when they collectively work together, the result is a spectacular, breathtaking display of sparkling beauty—a complexity of dazzling, vibrant color too magnificent for words.

Picture God's glory residing in the core of this crystal prism. We cannot see His glory inside, yet we know it's there. All we can see are the little facets of beauty that shimmer around the perimeter of the prism, reflecting the glory within. As a whole, this prism reflects God's inner glory so brightly as to render us speechless in reverent awe. Its brilliance defies the human tongue; it cannot begin to be defined or described with words. In His grace, He lovingly reveals the brilliant splendor of His glory to us one facet at a time—it's all we can handle!

This book is a compilation of fifty chapters, each representing one of the many crystal faces on the prism that comprise the whole. Each face shines with a unique and dazzling luster, portraying a slightly different facet of God's glory. We must intentionally live with our eyes wide open so we don't miss glimpses of His glory shimmering all around us.

As we delve into each chapter together, may we come closer to understanding what it means to reflect God's glory in its full splendor, majesty, and grandeur. Please forgive me if I have trivialized His glory. I realize the word picture of a prism is woefully inadequate. His glory is abundantly more exquisite, breathtaking, and magnificent than any prism our eyes have ever seen.

The Glory of God

"Our ultimate aim in life is not to be
healthy, wealthy, prosperous, or problem free.
Our ultimate aim in life is to bring glory to God."[A]

Anne Graham Lotz

"The glory of God shines, indeed,
in all creatures on high and below,
but never more brightly than in the cross."

John Calvin

"Seek not your own glory.
Seek God
and his glory will be seen in you,
radiant in humility and
in the strength of his might
made manifest even in your brokenness."[B]

Douglas McKelvey

1

∾

Reflecting His Glory

The word for *glory* comes from a Hebrew word, kābôd, which means weighty or heavy. It was originally used in monetary transactions. Precious metals, such as gold and silver were weighed and used as currency. The heavier the metal, the more valuable it was. This later evolved into the word we know as *glory*. So, when we speak of the glory of God, we are expressing the value or worth of God.[A]

When referring to God, His glory cannot be adequately defined; it can only be experienced. In our feeble attempts to capture it with words, we stumble around the sacred and stammer in its presence; glory cannot be tamed by our mortal tongues. We may pursue it by reading the Bible, only to find its power and truths bubble up and drench each page. His glory cannot be controlled nor contained.

Glory isn't only an attribute of God—a part of who He is. It is all of God—His totality. It encompasses His greatness, His holiness, His power, His perfection. God created us for His glory.[1] As such, Dr. John Piper tells us, "The deepest longing of the human heart is to know and enjoy the glory of God. We were made for this."[B] We ache to be filled with the glory of God.

Created in the image of God, humanity is wired to notice and savor the glory of God. So, we embrace the glorious in our world as we seek to satisfy this innate hunger that drives us:

- the untouched beauty of the sun cresting over rugged, majestic, snow-chiseled mountains
- an enthralling piece of musical genius
- the gentleness of dawn painting the sky in festive hues
- the breathtaking grandeur of autumn's tapestry ablaze in vivid color
- the pure sweetness of a baby's uncontained giggle
- the gentle elegance of a delicate snowfall gracefully transforming the once barren brown landscape into a magical spectacle of pristine beauty
- the wondrous magnetic pull of the ocean accentuated by crashing waves against the shore
- the incredible diversity of vegetation and wildlife
- the vastness of sky erupting with the fiery outburst of the setting sun
- the ear-splitting clap of thunder as a flash of lightning zigzags with uncontrolled fury across the inky night sky
- the full rainbow, shining its finery of iridescent colors, claiming the expanse of sky above

John Stonestreet and Shane Morris suggest, "Every star, every flower, and every grain of sand is also charged with divine truth…Every earthly beauty is a reflection of a heavenly reality."[C] God is the divine artist and intentionally shares His glory with us! The whole Earth is filled with His glory and every magnificent display reflects God—the Creator and Source of glory! He is the only One who can satisfy our hunger. Everyone, no matter where they live, knows God to some degree through His glory on display.[2]

As we embrace His glory, we are set ablaze from within. We reflect the light of His glory with blinding intensity by the way we live, as a mirror reflects an image.[3]

> As water reflects the face,
> so one's life reflects the heart.
> Proverbs 27:19

The light within pierces and shatters the darkness around us and God is on display. Our lives become a testimony of His goodness and power—and people are drawn to the light. In this way, we impact the culture—and the world—with eternal consequences that bring glory to God.

One day, on the other side of Heaven, we will see and experience the vibrant fullness of God's splendor and glory in its purest sense. It will take our breath away! All we will be able to do is praise Him!

And we will never be the same!

---

[1] Isaiah 43:7 – whom I created for my glory.

[2] Romans 1:20b, NLT – Through everything God made, they can clearly see his invisible qualities—his eternal power and divine nature.

[3] 2 Corinthians 3:18b, TLB – We can be mirrors that brightly reflect the glory of the Lord.

2

⁓

Boomerang Blessing

The first book in this series, *Living for His Glory*, was about living in a way that brings glory to God. Now let's take it a step further. When we lovingly and intentionally live for His glory, God's hope is that we will reflect this glory to the watching world.

As an example, let's take a look at the Sun and its power. It is a fiery sphere of self-generating, self-sustaining burning plasma and gases—the only star in our solar system. Temperatures top 27 million degrees Fahrenheit.[A] Every second it converts 600 million tons of hydrogen into helium, emitting light and energy into space.[B]

The largest object in our solar system, the Sun weighs 333,000 times as much as the Earth; 1.3 million Earths could fit inside it.[C] The Sun is 93,000,000 miles from Earth.[D] The speed of light travels at 186,000 miles/second, yet it takes eight minutes and 20 seconds for a ray of sunlight to reach Earth.[E]

A car traveling 65 mph would take just over 163 years to reach the Sun. A man walking at a brisk pace of 4 mph—never stopping—would take over 2654 years to reach the Sun. Outfitted in a highly protective space suit, an astronaut can only travel as close as 3 million miles to the Sun before burning to death.[G]

God is unapproachable light

In a powerful sermon on the glory of God, Dr. Tony Evans stated, "The Sun is God's illustration...of unapproachable light."[1] The Sun is our physical light whereas Jesus is our spiritual light—"the light of the world."[1] Like the Sun, God is also unapproachable light as no one can see God and live.[2]

> God...alone is immortal
> and...lives in unapproachable light,
> whom no one has seen or can see.
> 1 Timothy 6:15-16

Consider the Moon

The Moon consists of a dark rocky composition with no power of its own to shine light. Yet we see it shining brightly in the night sky. How is this possible? The Sun shines its light into space. Its rays hit the Moon and reflect off the surface; we can see this reflection from Earth. Although dark on its own, the Moon appears to have light due to the way it reflects the Sun's light.

The Sun and the Moon both "give" light, just in different ways. The Sun generates its own light, and the Moon reflects the light from the Sun. Jesus, the Son, shines His light (and glory) in our lives. But unlike the Moon, we have a choice. We can either absorb the light or reflect it.

When we live for ourselves

When we live with ourselves as the center of our universe, I call this living for the *little g* glory of self. Living in this manner puffs us up with a false sense of self-importance. As God's light and glory shine on us...

- we absorb all the goodness and blessings of God, taking full credit for our achievements and talents.
- we absorb His divine light and glory without shining it outward.

When people see us living for ourselves, they don't see God and His glory—His light. They simply see us—darkness—and not much else. Our *little g* glory is insignificant. It only elevates us in our own eyes (and maybe in the eyes of some OTHER people—for a short time). This glory is fleeting.

When we die and are buried, our *little g* glory is buried with us as it contains no power. People soon forget us; it's wasted glory. A wasted life.

When referencing the success of another, a friend recently told me, "She's in her glory!" Her *little g* glory had her trapped in its bubble—a dangerous place to be. This person sought her own glory. And found it. She also soon discovered that the joy of her own glory was shallow and short-lived.

When we live for God

When we walk with God and submit to His will, I call this living for the *big G* glory of God. This means we live in obedience to Him—with integrity—in a way that magnifies and honors Him. Our mindset is focused on the eternal, not the things of this world. As God's light and glory shine on us and we receive them…

- we reflect God's goodness and blessings outward, not taking credit for our achievements and talents.
- we reflect His light and glory into the darkness as we shine His holiness.

When people notice us living for God, they see the light of Christ working in us with divine power, transforming us into the image of Christ—into holiness. In this way, we reflect His *big G* glory outward to the world.

When we die, His glory lives on because this glory is eternal; it transcends our lives. Let it be said about you, "They're in His glory!"

An illustration

We have solar lights in front of our house lining the sidewalk. During the day, they absorb the light and energy of the sun so they can shine the light when the sun sets.

Over time, the light from the lamps fades. Bright at midnight. Not as much at 3am. Quite dim at 6am. The longer the solar lights are away from the sun, the dimmer they become.

Just like us.

When we spend time with God, we absorb the light of His glory, but as we get caught up in the world and its priorities, spending less time with God, the light of His glory fades with time—until we don't notice God's glory much anymore. The longer we are away from God, the less we reflect His light and glory; we don't shine so brightly.

Boomerang blessing

When we drink in God's energy and glory—living for God—we are transformed. With ever-increasing glory!

> We all, who with unveiled faces contemplate
> the Lord's glory, are being transformed into
> his image with ever-increasing glory,
> which comes from the Lord, who is the Spirit.
> 2 Corinthians 3:18

As we stay under His Lordship, we reflect His presence and power out to the world. Like our solar lights. And it turns our lives upside down! It's radical. Author Julia Loren states,

> Those who shine with the glory of God are destined to become walking spiritual experiences for others. Those who covet being in His presence, soak in His love, quiet their souls and allow the Lord to change them, become transformed…from glory to glory.

This is a boomerang blessing.

But that's not all!

We reflect His glory, not only out to the world, but right back to God! This is one way we glorify God—by reflecting His glory outward as a witness **and** upward as worship.

How about you?

As God shines the light of His glory and power in your life, will you absorb it or reflect it to a world living in darkness? And most importantly, will you reflect this glory back to God? It's a choice between an eternally significant life or a wasted life. Our choice reveals the essence of our soul and resonates throughout eternity with profound impact.

---

[1] John 8:12

[2] Exodus 33:20 – No one may see me and live.

3

Your Roots Matter

Groves of gigantic redwood trees grow from southern Oregon to northern California. These giants are absolutely massive, often soaring to well over 350 feet in height and weighing upwards of 500 tons.[A] Some are so large, 20 feet or more in diameter, that ten people can link hands and still not encircle the base.[B]

One would think these trees are deeply rooted to support the weight of their enormous structures. But what's fascinating is their very shallow root structure; their roots only grow into the soil about 6-12 feet—enough to get the water they need. A strong wind would blow one over if standing alone on a hillside.[A]

These gentle giants have a secret. They grow close together so that their roots not only grow down, but also extend more than 100 feet from the base so they intertwine with the roots of other redwoods. This creates a strong foundation and support system as they essentially lock together.[C] Despite a shallow root system, they are very resilient. When winds rage, earthquakes shake, and rains turn to floods, these trees stand strong—some for over 2000 years.[A]

We, too, grow our roots down into the soil of our lives. But the water we tap into is the living water and life-giving nourishment of the Holy Spirit that flows through us as we live out our faith.

"Whoever believes in me…
rivers of living water will flow
from within them."
John 7:38

Like these giant redwoods, we are easily threatened by the winds of discouragement and fear when we are alone. God purposely designed us for relationship. We thrive best in spiritual community—in the grove of caring and compassionate Christian friends.

We grow our roots not just down, but also out to the side to interweave with those of other believers as we share resources, pray for one another, and shoulder the burdens of life together. Friends like these help us stand strong when storms rage and winds of adversity bluster across our path. Solomon noted,

If either of them falls down,
one can help the other up.
But pity anyone who falls
and has no one to help them up.
Ecclesiastes 4:10

When we interweave our roots like this, we gain the collective strength of all the roots working together. It is part of God's grand design from the beginning. God, working in the context of the Trinity, created us in His image. Relationship—it's healthy. It's also necessary for us to perform at our best.

Our friends are His gift to us!

Like Jesus

The analogy of the grove of redwood trees paints a powerful word picture, yet it is limited. Like most analogies, we can only take it so far. Let's look at Jesus for further insight.

Jesus was firmly grounded in His relationship with His Father. He often retreated to be alone with Him, drawing strength from the bond they shared. He pursued God's will above all else and was fully surrendered to His plan.

In the same vein, we need to be anchored into the bedrock of a strong Christian faith—strengthened by reading God's Word, studying our Bible, and praying. There's an African proverb that states, "When the roots are deep, there is no reason to fear the wind."

Relationships were also very important to Jesus; He beautifully modeled the type of community we desperately need. Jesus encircled Himself with close friends (His disciples) with whom He enjoyed meals, served, shared His faith, and extended His love.

Biblical friendships (rooted in and built upon the foundation of Christ) are powerful. The world, ruled by Satan, will always pull us down. Interconnecting with a strong network of friends helps hold us up.

> Though one may be overpowered,
> two can defend themselves.
> Ecclesiastes 4:12

Jesus perfectly demonstrated how to grow a vertical root system anchored in God—as well as a horizontal root system intertwined with godly friends. This root system will give us the necessary strength to withstand the assaults of this world.

Look around you

With what kind of friends have you surrounded yourself? Are they the kind who are in for the long haul? Godly friends grow their roots into the soil of their community to help them stand strong. They believe in qualities that endure—characteristics such as honor, integrity, respect, commitment, love, and dignity.

> "God never intended that we be autonomous,
> living in our own personal faith.
> We are not like a bag of marbles;
> rather, we're to be like a bunch of grapes
> whose juices blend in times of pressure."[D]
> Dr. Charles Stanley

Plant yourself next to people who are grounded in faith and find ways to connect with them. Intentionally devote time to develop and solidify these vital friendships.

Storms will come

The winds will howl and threaten. Storms are inevitable. How solid is your root system—both vertically and horizontally?

- Is it anchored into the bedrock of Christ?
- Are your friendships built upon biblical truths you can count on when the going gets tough?

What kind of friend are you? You will find, with the right friends and support network, you will not only survive the most challenging trials, but rise above them.

Your roots matter.

4

Out on a Limb

We don't come across many people by the name of Zacchaeus. Not only is his name difficult to spell, but in Jesus's day, he was hated and rejected because he was a chief tax collector. Tax collectors had the authority to tax the people above and beyond the official tax set by the Roman officials; they kept the surplus for themselves. It's not hard to see why tax collectors were shunned and despised. As the chief tax collector, Zacchaeus supervised many tax collectors.

One day changed everything for Zacchaeus. What a day it was! He had heard of a man named Jesus. Everyone was talking about Him. He was performing many miracles; it was astounding! Could the rumors be true? One day, he learned that this miracle-working man was walking to Jerusalem and would pass through his hometown: Jericho. Zacchaeus was eager to catch a glimpse of Him. And he wasn't the only one. A large crowd had gathered for the same reason; they all wanted to see Jesus.

Knowing he could never get to the front of the throngs of people and too short to see over the sea of heads, Zacchaeus devised a plan. He ran to a nearby sycamore-fig tree and climbed it. He went out on a limb—literally—to get a good view! There he was, hanging out over the crowd on a branch—a highly undignified position for a man of his standing! He must have been curious enough—lonely enough—empty enough—to be this desperate. (In that culture, grown men did not run, nor climb trees.)

Craning his neck to see what all the hubbub was about, Zacchaeus must have been quite excited when he finally caught sight of Jesus trudging up the road. He watched as Jesus came closer and closer…

Suddenly time stood still as Jesus stopped just below the branch on which Zacchaeus was perched. Then, lo and behold, He looked up. Jesus noticed him and called to him—not with contempt, but with kindness. Jesus didn't comment on what a detestable sinner he was. Instead, Jesus recognized him by name with a charge. "Zacchaeus, come down immediately. I must stay at your house today."[1] Not what Zacchaeus expected to hear by a long shot. He was stunned! On His way to carry out the most important mission in human history (our salvation), Jesus found time to care about a single lost soul!

Imagine how Zacchaeus must have felt. Living as a miserable sinner. Alone. Scorned. Wealthy, yet spiritually bankrupt. Rejected by the masses yet accepted by the Son of God—the only One who mattered!

Although small in stature, Zacchaeus was big on humbling himself by climbing a tree to learn more. Seeing Jesus was more important to him than maintaining his dignity. He didn't mind being ridiculed if it meant seeing this miracle man.

At Jesus's command, he jumped down, greeted Him with joy, and made a radical proclamation: "Lord! Here and now I give half of my possessions to the poor, and if I have cheated anybody out of anything, I will pay back four times the amount."[2]

From brash to benevolent—cruel to kind. From unloving to loving—crass to caring. Jesus transforms lives!

When we devote our lives to the glory of God, our lives carry divine significance and leave eternal marks.

Who is in the crowd around you?

Every single day, we pass by or interact with people who are "up a tree" or "out on a limb" trying to figure out life—trying to determine what makes Christ-followers different. As Christians, we reflect the light of God's glory. And people notice. Sometimes they hang back and watch us from a distance. Sometimes they are bolder. We may not even be aware of them as we go about our business, preoccupied with our tasks at hand.

All around us, people are making tragic decisions that will impact the rest of their lives—and beyond. And yet, they don't know any other way to live. They live empty, unhappy, lonely, unfulfilled lives, desperate for the hope of something better.

We are called to stand in the gap

- to look for those who are hanging out on the fringes of the crowd.
- to recognize those who are seeking, although maybe not consciously.
- to reach out and engage with those who admit they are lacking something.

No matter our physical height—or our spiritual height—we, like Zacchaeus, come up short...short of the glory of God.[3] Yet Jesus seeks us out, just as He did with Zacchaeus. The Bible tells us Jesus stands patiently and persistently knocking at the door of our hearts—hoping we will open up and invite Him in.[4] He longs for us to be willing to go out into the world reflecting the confident hope and joy of our salvation.

Let's patiently seek and call out to those who might realize their smallness in spirit and risk going out on a limb to discover the secret to filling their spiritual void.

- Let's pray for the opportunity to usher in Christ in a way others can understand and embrace.
- Let's pray for the softening of hearts so they can see their desperate need and receive the message.
- Let's resolve not to be so busy that we miss lost souls. May lives be transformed (as the life of this desperate tax collector long ago) when they encounter Christ.

Be prepared to glorify God with the harvest—as new believers respond to Christ with joy, turning their greed to generosity—just as Zacchaeus did!

---

[1] Luke 19:5b

[2] Luke 19:8

[3] Romans 3:23 – All have sinned and fall short of the glory of God.

[4] Revelation 3:20, CEV – Listen! I am standing and knocking at your door. If you hear my voice and open the door, I will come in and we will eat together.

5

⚬∽

The Cockeyed Squid

God created so many unusual animals for us to discover and enjoy. I imagine He is delighted when we explore and uncover something that fascinates us and satisfies our quest for the bizarre and peculiar.

The cockeyed squid would qualify. It is one quirky creature that lives in the ocean's twilight zone. The ocean is divided into three zones based on the depth of the water and amount of sunlight that can penetrate. The middle zone is called the twilight zone and is between 660 and 3300 feet (200 to 1000 meters) deep. It is the lowest level of the ocean that light is able to reach.[A] This is where the cockeyed squid lives.[B] The lowest zone is immersed in inky blackness[A] as sunlight cannot penetrate at all.

This squid is born with two identical eyes, but as it grows and matures, the left eye rapidly swells in size, growing to more than twice the size of the right eye by adulthood! It also transforms into a semi-tubular shape with a prominent yellow lens.[B] The right eye remains small and black; it may even shrivel a bit with age.[C] Duke University marine biologist Kate Thomas states, "No other mollusk is so mismatched. No other bilaterally symmetrical animals are known to exhibit two distinct, or dimorphic, eyeballs."[B] First discovered in the late 1800s, researchers have been puzzled as to the reason for this anomaly until recently.[B]

In its natural habitat, scientists have observed that the cockeyed squid consistently swims in an odd, upside-down position—head down, tail up. The larger left eye faces slightly upward toward the sunlight filtering down from above. It picks up shadows from the sun shining down through the water which helps it discern marine life swimming overhead. The smaller right eye faces slightly downward, searching for bioluminescence, the only source of light below.

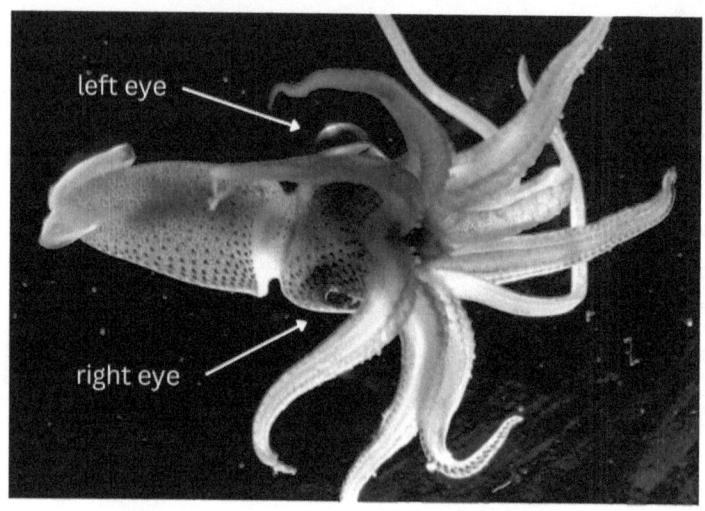

left eye

right eye

aa

A different type of eye structure is needed to distinguish glowing fish from the dark water below as the squid searches for potential meals and predators.[C] The unusual yellow lens is simply an effective camouflage technique.[B]

Let's face it: The cockeyed squid is a quirky guy! Yet, it is able to navigate its complex and often threatening environment.

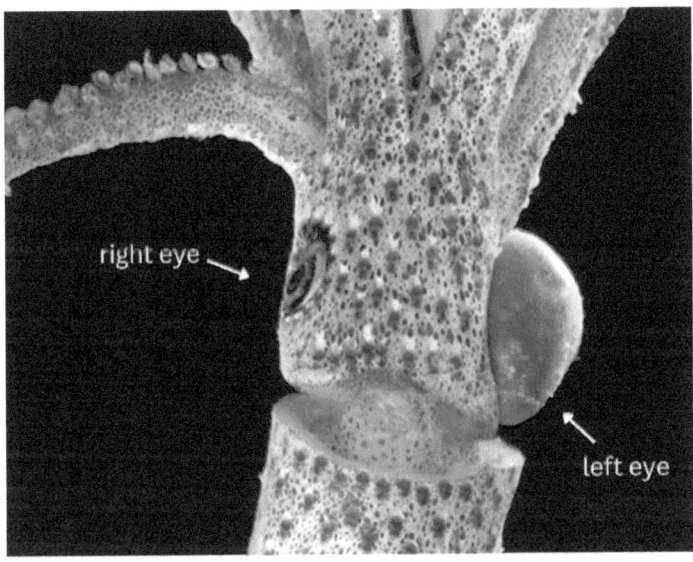

right eye

left eye

bb

Living cockeyed

This peculiar squid poses an intriguing illustration of how we are to live with one eye on our physical world and one eye focused toward Heaven. With one eye trained on what's happening around us, we seek to live in a way that glorifies and reflects God. We discern what is healthy and what threatens our spiritual survival as we strive to live righteously, serve with love, and reach out to those who are lost and in need of a greater hope.

With a larger eye trained heavenward, we will be more sensitive to what's happening spiritually in the light of eternity. This will help us prioritize the eternal over the temporal, aware that God is continuously working in the spiritual realm for our good and His glory.

Knowing our true home is in Christ gives us a distinctly different perspective on life than the non-believer. The more we set our minds on eternal things, the more we seek what God desires.

Set your hearts on things above, where Christ is,
seated at the right hand of God.
Set your minds on things above,
not on earthly things.
Colossians 3:1b-2

This gives us peace and joy as we live in a world with sin and suffering—a world in which we don't belong. A different kind of eye is needed to see through the darkness of our world. To be able to discern threats and predators, like the squid, we must swim wisely as we navigate the cultural waters. As we find identity in Him, our eternal salvation is secure.

Your life is now hidden with Christ in God.
When Christ, who is your life, appears,
then you also will appear with him in glory.
Colossians 3:3b-4

He provides us strength to live in our twilight zone—the dark waters of our world. He gives us a sure hope of the future, anchored in His promise to return one day soon to take us to our eternal home. When He calls us home, we will ascend from our twilight zone into the brilliant, pure light of His glory where we will receive new bodies—and new eyes—for eternity.

Until then, let's keep an eye on the eastern sky. He's coming soon. Let's not miss Him.

One more thing

I'm sure some people think we're quirky. So be it. Like the cockeyed squid, we are simply being who God created us to be!

6

Never Say Never

You must admire his enthusiasm. He loved His Lord and yearned to be more faithful to Him than any of the other disciples. Yet, I doubt he realized just how difficult this would prove to be. Ah…Peter…he meant well.

During His last supper with His disciples, Jesus tried to prepare them for what was about to happen. He even predicted that Judas would betray Him. After eating, they walked together to the Mount of Olives. There Jesus informed them that they would abandon Him—all of them. This greatly upset Peter; he vehemently denied this would ever happen. Jesus zeroed in on him and told him that within hours, Peter would indeed disown Him. Not once, but three times! And it would happen "this very night before the rooster crows."[1]

Never say never

Events unfolded precisely as Jesus warned. He and His disciples walked to the Garden of Gethsemane. Judas approached Him with a large crowd sent by the chief priests and elders. It was here Judas betrayed Jesus with evil intent.

The men brusquely seized and arrested Jesus. Watching with unmitigated horror, the disciples were overcome with fear and confusion—and they bolted, deserting Jesus when it mattered most. Fear makes us do things we would never otherwise do. The men took Jesus to Caiaphas, the high priest.

Peter, afraid but curious, didn't take off with the other disciples, but unobtrusively followed from a distance to watch what was happening. He decided to hang out in the courtyard of Caiaphas, keeping a low profile, while he observed and listened to those around him.

It was then that a servant girl entered and was startled to see Peter in the flickering glow of the courtyard fire. "You also were with Jesus of Galilee."[2] Peter shook his head rapidly, denying the accusation. "I don't know what you're talking about."[3] Peter nervously left and quickly walked out to the gateway where another girl saw him, making the same observation as the first. Growing increasingly anxious, Peter vehemently denied it again, "I don't know the man!"[4]

Others were standing there and wouldn't let it rest! With an impassioned outburst, a servant of the high priest pressed the issue with Peter. "Surely you are one of them; your accent gives you away."[5] With beads of sweat collecting on his upper brow, Peter trembled as he fervently denied Jesus yet again.

Immediately, the silence that followed was shattered by the shrill, piercing crow of a rooster.

Recalling Jesus's prediction, combined with the realization of what just transpired, Peter's eyes grew wide with horror and shame. He broke down and wept. Crushed and defeated, Peter was inconsolable; he realized that in fear, he denied that he was indeed a follower of Jesus Christ.

He had three chances, and he blew it every—single—time!

(Please read the story in Matthew 26:31-35, 69-75.)

This could have been avoided

Peter had been duly warned. Warned by the One he most revered and trusted. Yet Peter chose the position of smug self-confidence instead of taking Jesus's warning seriously. He boasted. If others might be tempted to stumble in their faithfulness, certainly not Peter! He didn't guard himself against temptation. In his brash cockiness, he stood vulnerable and unprotected.

Peter had followed Jesus at a distance. Half-heartedly. Not enough to claim allegiance to Him, yet enough to casually keep a curious eye on Him.

Is it possible you follow Jesus in this manner? You nonchalantly keep track of Jesus, yet not enough to claim you share a loyalty. Not enough to defend Him or risk your reputation for Him.

Don't you think Peter would have been looking out for roosters? (Back then, roosters commonly roamed the towns.) "Has anyone seen any roosters? Because if so, I'm outta here. Jesus mentioned a rooster might be around."

Nope. His mind wasn't on roosters; it should have been. The rooster would be God's warning siren. (Of interest, the rooster is sometimes used as a symbol of human weakness and Christ's grace in forgiving sinners. It can also represent watchfulness.[A])

Peter didn't act wisely; he was distracted, too wrapped up in his own agenda. He had three chances—yet he failed. He could have walked away unscathed. Instead, he was pulled deeper and deeper into the clutches of temptation to compromise. We would be wise to learn from his downfall. The only person safe from temptation is the one who flees from it.

Peter chose to hang out in the wrong place with the wrong people at the wrong time. He lied by denying any association with Jesus not once, but three times in a row. Peter conceded his principles so he wouldn't attract the attention of those who had seized Jesus. By surrounding himself with the wrong people, he ended up doing the wrong things.

What's even more tragic is that Peter likely recalled this scene each morning for the rest of his life—every daybreak when he heard a rooster crow. Living with regret is a dreadful thing.

Little by little

On the slope of Long's Peak in Colorado, a massive tree had stood for 400 years, only to crash to the ground one day. Everyone was totally baffled as this tree had survived avalanches, countless storms over four centuries, and fourteen lightning strikes.

It turned out the tree had been killed by beetles.[B] These insects had chewed their way through its mighty fibers little by little over a prolonged period of time. This is how compromise works. Satan doesn't tell you what he is up to. Instead, he comes to you with a little enticement. He torments you bit by bit by infiltrating your walls of principle through compromise. He takes you down one bite at a time as he chisels his way through your integrity.

Let's get personal

If someone like Peter can fail, we can certainly fail more readily. After all, Peter spent three years of his life in daily fellowship with Jesus. Surely, he learned something of value by watching, following, and sharing life with Him. Yet, when the chips were down, he didn't want to stand out among pagans, so he compromised in order to fit in.

When you allow others to lower your standards, you will easily be drawn into sin. Are you in any relationships like this—hanging out with the wrong people? Perhaps a romance? Or a close friendship? Do you hesitate to declare your allegiance to the Lord lest you offend someone? Or stand out? Are you compromising your principles and beliefs? Do you risk your integrity when you're with certain people? Are you afraid of what others will think if you tell them "No"?

Learn from Peter. Before being filled with the Holy Spirit at Pentecost, he denied His Lord three times—even after promising to follow Him to the death! But after being filled with the Spirit, He spoke boldly and confidently to the Jews at Pentecost. And thousands came to faith. It was Peter's confession of faith on which Jesus later built His Church.[6]

Temptations are common—so common, in fact, that Paul issues us a warning—to choose our friends carefully, for we will unwittingly conform to their standards without even realizing it.[7] Be careful where you hang out. Be cautious with whom you spend your time. Non-believers may naturally lead you away from the things of Christ, often without realizing it, which can cause your faith to falter.

Don't make yourself vulnerable by sporting the smug swagger Peter did. Jesus is not impressed with foolhardy bluster. Don't be brash in declaring your inability to sin in a particular area. That's exactly where you will be tempted to be led astray. Jesus knows us better than we know ourselves. He knows what tempts us and will always provide an escape.[8]

Never say never.

If you have been noncommittal and half-hearted in your relationship with Jesus, following at a safe distance, today is the day that can change. Step up and boldly declare your faithfulness to Jesus. No matter what. Joshua, the man God chose to lead the Israelites into the Promised Land, said it best: "Choose for yourselves this day whom you will serve...But as for me and my household, we will serve the LORD."[9] Following Jesus demands bold faith. It's risky, yet well worth it.

Christians have been accused of being intolerant and narrow-minded. Instead of standing strong for the gospel, we apologize for the Bible and its positions on cultural issues. We compromise our faith to appease the world and not appear intolerant. The enemy has gained access to the Church through the crumbling fibers of the living tissue within and is doing all he can to bring it crashing down. The Church is conforming to the world.

Stand your ground

Be absolutely certain your allegiance to the Lord directs and orders your life—no matter who you're around. Protect your integrity. Shield and defend the Church. At all costs! And for Pete's sake (pun intended), keep an eye out for roosters!

---

[1] Matthew 26:34
[2] Matthew 26:69
[3] Matthew 26:70
[4] Matthew 26:72
[5] Matthew 26:73
[6] Matthew 16:18 – You are Peter, and on this rock [of your confession of faith] I will build my church. (Brackets mine.)
[7] 1 Corinthians 15:33b – Bad company corrupts good character.
[8] 1 Corinthians 10:13b – God is faithful...when you are tempted, he will also provide a way out.
[9] Joshua 24:15

7

Free Fall

My eyes were riveted on my husband. Bob's expression was one of unwavering resolve as he gripped the rigid steel bar above his head for all he was worth. With methodical precision, the brawny man standing behind him slowly and forcefully peeled each of Bob's fingers from the bar, gradually loosening his grip.

With nervous tension, I held my breath as I watched the scene unfold before me from a short distance away. I was unable to communicate, nor offer help. As soon as the man managed to get one hand free, he focused on the other hand. As he did so, Bob reached out for the steel bar again with his free hand, tenaciously taking hold in a desperate attempt to regain control. Yet, the man was determined.

Finally, he freed both of Bob's hands and in one swift motion, forced Bob out of the plane which was soaring at 12,000 feet in the air. Bob found himself in a sudden free fall, with the man securely strapped to his back in his first skydiving experience.

I was next. Then our daughter.

The dive

If you've never been skydiving, let me try to put into words what it feels like to jump from a plane and hurtle toward Earth. It was an exhilarating blur of sensations to be plummeting through the sky, free falling at 120 miles per hour as gravity took control. Adrenaline surged, and every fiber of my being was alive with the heart-pounding thrill of the moment.

First of all, it's cold—really cold. The temperature drops about 10°F for every 3000 feet. So at 12,000 feet, it was about 40°F colder than on the ground.[A] Since it was Thanksgiving weekend, the temperature at that altitude was probably in the 20°s. Brrr!

The wind resistance hit surprisingly hard and felt like a massive force, against which I was totally powerless. Imagine driving down the expressway at 60mph while hanging out the window. Now double that! Panic quickly overtook me; I felt myself suffocating, an intense pressure against my face, as I struggled to inhale the bitter cold oxygen! We were told if we screamed when this panic sensation struck, we would know with assurance we were breathing. So, I screamed!

The intense rush of wind created a deafening, roaring noise. Conversing with the man on my back was literally impossible! It was disorienting as the horizon tilted and spun as if in a dizzying dream.

As we descended, the ground below gradually came into focus. After about 50-60 seconds of free fall, my tandem instructor pulled the ripcord, and the parachute deployed and unfurled above us, engulfing the air with a palpable hunger. Our descent slowed from 120mph to 20mph in about five seconds.[B] It was jolting—like someone engaged the brakes—hard! The chaotic free fall to floating descent was both exhilarating and serene. The initial sensation was one of floating upward, but it was deceptive—as we were still falling. Then—it suddenly became very quiet—almost eerie. Surreal.

Swinging beneath the canopy of the parachute for the next four to seven minutes is, quite unexpectedly, almost soothing. It was as if the world stopped spinning and came to a standstill. Because there isn't significant change in the acceleration of the descent, the sensation of the free fall still mimics floating or flying, not falling.

I gaped in wonder as I shifted my focus from survival instincts to the breathtaking beauty of God's vast creation exploding in full glory from all directions! I saw the world with profound clarity from a radically new perspective—with only air between me and the earth. I took in the intricate mosaic of the landscape below—patches of lush green grass, winding rivers, and structures of civilization resembling a child's toys. At that altitude, all earthly smells are absent. As I descended, I smelled nothing—just fresh, pure, crisp air. It was humbling, invigorating, and refreshing.

The ground soon surged upward to welcome my approach. And before I knew it, I was back on the ground as a swell of triumph washed over me. I gazed skyward at the vast blue expanse that had been my playground for this extraordinary escapade. As I paused to reflect, I marveled at what had just transpired—wondering if I dreamed it all!

Our personal free fall

When a crisis grips us, it's as if we lost our grip and are being shoved out of an airplane soaring at 12,000 feet. We enter our own personal free fall. We try to grasp that which should be secure but find we can't hold on; nothing in our world is trustworthy. We tumble in an emotional free fall at an alarming rate. It can be terrifying! It feels like an intense wind in our face creating massive pressure. We may panic, feeling we can't breathe, as anxiety takes control.

We are in survival mode. We reach for the ripcord and deploy our parachute.

What is your parachute? Where do you turn in a crisis? Do you pick up the phone? Do you drown your worries in alcohol, food, TV, or the internet to distract yourself from having to cope? All these coping mechanisms can help blunt the pain and distract us for a bit, but they don't do much to curb the free fall.

Only one parachute can help bring your free fall under control—your faith. When you deploy this parachute, you regain stability. You can look around and better survey the landscape—assess the situation. You feel a sense of calm knowing you can trust your parachute—your faith—because the object of your faith is God. You can breathe again as you reassess your world, gliding under the canopy of your faith. You can even relax a little as you are carried safely from one moment to the next.

Please don't misunderstand me—you're still in a free fall, which is more than a bit unnerving. You don't know when or how you'll land, but you find the landscape of your new world is now in much better focus. As you pray, a quiet hush wraps you in a peaceful embrace.

Because of your faith in a holy and sovereign God, you know you will survive and you're not alone; Jesus is the man on your back. He is closer than close. You can relax because He is in control, and He is trustworthy.

As people watch you, they won't understand how you're holding it together. Peace is your companion as you reflect your Savior—the Prince of Peace. Although your world is in chaos, there is still beauty to be found. You will get through this.

8

~⁓∾⁓~

Sheep in Human Clothing

Throughout the Bible, Jesus often compares us to sheep, identifying Himself as our loving Shepherd. "When he saw the crowds, he had compassion on them, because they were harassed and helpless, like sheep without a shepherd."[1] In our society, we rarely see sheep, so we can't appreciate the significance of this comparison.

But in the days of Christ, people were very familiar with sheep, shepherds, and shepherding, so they well understood all the references. Shepherding is still a vital industry in Israel today. While in Israel, my family and I saw many shepherds tending their flocks. Let's explore the attributes and peculiarities of sheep alongside the nature of the sheep-shepherd relationship to better understand how Jesus's statements are just as relevant to us today.

Let's talk sheep

Of all domesticated animals, sheep need the most care and are the most helpless. They spend their entire day grazing, wandering from place to place, never looking up. They rarely even look to their shepherd. As a result, they often get lost[2] and are far too disoriented to find their way home. Sheep have no sense of direction or "homing instinct" as many other animals do.[A] They must wait to be rescued. "So will I look after my sheep. I will rescue them from all the places where they were scattered."[3]

- How many of us foolishly spend our days grazing from place to place, never finding the time to look up? We race from one errand to the next, our heads down, lost in our phones, projects, and to-do lists. We are self-absorbed from sunrise to sunset, barely able to steal a moment to look up at the beauty of our world or to notice other people in our path, much less our Shepherd. When we do look up, we are often disoriented and detached from the world around us. We feel lost. How long has it been since we've opened the Bible? Days have gone by; we have drifted far from our Shepherd—our anchor. Like sheep, our homing instinct is lacking; we have a hard time finding our way back.

Sheep are dumb, foolish, and gullible. They are easily influenced by a crowd. It isn't unusual for a sheep to wander to the edge of a cliff and fall off. The story is told of 1500 sheep who jumped off a cliff in Turkey simply because one sheep fell over the edge and plunged 50 feet to its death! Their strong instinct to follow a leader, without thought of danger, often leads to their destruction.[B] In jest, someone once said, "The hardest part of trying to steal one sheep is stopping the rest of them from following."

- Oh, that peer pressure! What a strong pull it is at every age! Truth be told, very few of us are actual leaders. If one person goes one way or leans in a certain direction, we often veer that way as well without thinking where we are heading…only to find ourselves in a mess!

Sheep are afraid of almost anything and are utterly defenseless against predators. If a wolf or bear approaches, the sheep don't try to run or spread out. They huddle together for safety and thus are easily caught.[B] But the shepherd has compassion[4] and will do everything within his power to protect his sheep, even giving his life for them.[5]

- Do you struggle with fear? Do you easily fall prey to a scam or an easy talker? Our antennae aren't up as they should be. People rein us in with their fast talking, their stories, or their ploys. We get taken. We get hurt. We don't have our spiritual armor on.

When thirsty, sheep tend to wander into running streams and immediately find themselves in a heap of trouble. Their wool quickly absorbs the water, weighing them down. Because they can't fight the current or move toward the edge quickly enough, they drown.[C] Shepherds only lead their beloved sheep to still water.

- On our own, we thirst for the things this world offers and may try drinking from dangerous moving waters and find ourselves drowning in a heap of trouble. We must look to our Great Shepherd to protect us by leading us to still waters.

aa

As a shepherd looks out over his flock, he knows each sheep by name, their unique preferences and proclivities, their dispositions and vulnerabilities.[D]

- Jesus, our Great Shepherd, knows each of us individually; He knows our names. He also knows our personal likes and tendencies, our personalities and weaknesses.

Shepherds are inseparable from their flocks. When the flocks commingle, the shepherd only needs to call his sheep; they recognize his voice[E] and follow him.[6]

- When we have commingled with other flocks, we can find our way back if we listen for His voice. If we have not learned to recognize His voice, we will be at great risk of injury. We must study our Bible and the character of Jesus, so we know His voice when He calls.

bb

In biblical times, when evening rolled around, the shepherd led his flock back to the sheep pen. He stood at the doorway, gave them a cool drink of water, and inspected each animal as it passed under his crook.[F] He knew sheep were susceptible to injuries. He removed thorns, treated lacerations, and applied soothing oil to their wounds.G The shepherd was a physician, as well as a guide and protector of his sheep.

- Jesus is well aware of our struggles and ailments— how we butt heads with others and get emotionally wounded. "You anoint my head with oil"7 describes how He applies the soothing oil (often a metaphor for the Holy Spirit) of comfort and encouragement to our wounds when we come to Him. He always knows what we need to be restored to wholeness. His tender compassion nurtures our trembling hearts.

Sheep are prone to disease and parasites. They are often besieged by dreadful little bot flies that enter their nostrils. They work their way up the nasal passages (sometimes all the way to the brain) and burrow in the flesh to lay their eggs, which hatch into maggots.H They torment the sheep mercilessly, causing them to thrash about, beating their heads against rocks to relieve the torture of the unrelenting itch and crawling sensations, sometimes causing their death. Their ears and eyes are also susceptible to aggravating insects which pester them ruthlessly. The sheep are powerless to free themselves of these wretched insects. Infection sets in, at times leading to blindness. To prevent this, the shepherd often anoints the entire head of each sheep with oil, creating a barrier of protection against these creatures. Then they have peace.I

- What torments you, causing you to beat your head against the wall? What anxious thoughts, fears, and obsessions grip you and won't let go, threatening to steal your sanity? Do you have times of mental torment? Pray for a fresh anointing of His Holy Spirit to grant a barrier of peace against the evil torment of the enemy—the annoyances of the world—that keep you distraught and anguished. May your cup overflow with His compassion, kindness, and protection. His blessings are endless.

There was no gate or physical door on the sheep pen—a crudely made rock enclosure, topped with thorns for protection. The shepherd kept the sheep in and wild animals out by lying across the opening all night. He slept there all night long, protecting them, literally becoming the door to the sheepfold.F No animal could pass in either direction without his knowledge.

- Jesus tells us, "I am the door; anyone who enters through Me will be saved [and will live forever]."8 A door creates division between the outside and the inside. Our Shepherd serves as the *door* between us and the outside world. Those who put their faith in Jesus as their Savior are inside the sheepfold. Those who place their faith in other things will find themselves outside the door of Jesus Christ. There is only one door through which to enter—to be protected—and to be saved.

The shepherd never abandons his sheep. He always scans the horizon, looking for potential attacks or to spot a meandering sheep. He doesn't hesitate to take on a bear or a lion if his sheep are in danger. He uses his rod and staff to protect, comfort, and guide them.E He compassionately seeks out the lone sheep to restore it to the flock. He risks his life to defend the sheep.9

- Weary and worn, weighed down by the worries of our world, we often meander without purpose or direction. Filled with compassion and love, Jesus always scans the horizon for potential threats, and He notices if we drift mindlessly about. He seeks us out when we've strayed and stands ready to carry us back to the fold, no matter how far we have roamed. "You were like sheep going astray, but now you have returned to the Shepherd...of your souls."[10]

cc

On their own, sheep have a hard time finding pasture for grazing and water. They'll eat anything, even poisonous weeds.[A] Without sufficient nutrition, they become weak and susceptible to illness. The shepherd guides them to verdant green pastures, rich with the nutrients he knows they need to be healthy and strong.[11]

- When we come to God each day in prayer and Bible reading, He renews our souls and provides us with the spiritual nourishment we need to face that day. When we skip this important spiritual discipline, we flounder and become spiritually depleted.

Enemies always wait to attack a flock of sheep; savage wolves were, and continue to be, a major threat.[12] Sheep have no claws, fangs, talons, quills, or venom to defend themselves; they won't fight. They have spindle legs and tiny hooves. They are awkward, weak, and pitifully slow.[B, J]

- We also face many enemies seeking our destruction (e.g. greed, pride, bitterness, selfishness). Men try to deceive us and cause us to stray from our faith. The enemy also pursues us; alone we are defenseless. Jesus is stronger than any enemy we will face. He fights for us, always protects us, and keeps us safe.[13] He assures us we will never perish.[14]

If a sheep ends up on its back, it struggles mightily to get back on its feet, especially if pregnant, overweight, or sporting a heavy fleece, perhaps laden with filth and muck; they need their shepherd to help them roll back over.[K]

- Are there times when life turns your world upside down? Are you weighed down with worries? Has something happened which took your feet right out from under you? You are immobilized, unable to get it together. You hardly know which end is up! But your Shepherd does. Don't withdraw in defeat and despair. He sees you and extends His hand. Together, you can walk out the challenge you're facing to get back on your feet. Acknowledge you're helpless without Him and surrender to His help.

Sheep have poor visual acuity directly in front of them and no depth perception. They can't see very far ahead.[L] They need a shepherd to guide them.

- Our spiritual vision is poor; we can't see clearly what lies ahead of us either. Everything is so unpredictable, and we don't know which way to turn. We need our Shepherd and His guidance.

Are you in the flock of Jesus? Your Shepherd cares for you and loves you fiercely. Keep your eyes on Him as you graze; He will lead you to green pastures and beside still waters as He restores your soul.[15] He knows you intimately and is with you always; He will comfort and encourage you when you stumble and struggle. He is the Great Physician; He heals the brokenhearted.[16,17] His goodness, peace, and joy will surround and sustain you. And one day He will carry you home to Heaven to live with Him forever.

The ultimate psalm about shepherding

Penned by David, Psalm 23 is his most famous psalm. He was a shepherd for years and knew the loving care he gave his sheep was like that he received from His Father.

The LORD is my shepherd; I shall not want.
He makes me lie down in green pastures.
He leads me beside still waters.

He restores my soul.
He leads me in paths of righteousness
for his name's sake.

Even though I walk through
the valley of the shadow of death,
I will fear no evil, for you are with me;
your rod and your staff, they comfort me.

You prepare a table before me
in the presence of my enemies;
you anoint my head with oil;
my cup overflows.

Surely goodness and mercy shall follow me
all the days of my life, and I shall
dwell in the house of the LORD forever.
Psalm 23, ESV

Our Shepherd knows us intimately and expects us to act like sheep. He doesn't expect us to behave like eagles or lions. He knows we wander off, ask dumb questions, follow wrong leaders, and frequently get ourselves into trouble. He doesn't admonish us for being stupid or thoughtless. He expects us to be sheep—and He loves us anyway.

I am so grateful to be in the sheepfold with you. Let's remember to thank Jesus for being our tender-hearted and devoted Shepherd and for loving us enough to give His life for us—His sheep.

As we graze together, remember to keep your head up and follow your adoring Shepherd; it is the only safe and peaceful place to be. And as you reflect your Shepherd, other sheep will watch and follow you into the fold of His loving mercy and grace.

[1] Matthew 9:36

[2] Isaiah 53:6 – We all, like sheep, have gone astray…

[3] Ezekiel 34:12b

[4] Matthew 9:36a – When he saw the crowds, he had compassion on them.

[5] John 10:11 – The good shepherd lays down his life for the sheep.

[6] John 10:4b – His sheep follow him because they know his voice.

[7] Psalm 23:5b

[8] John 10:9a, AMP

[9] 1 Samuel 17:34b-35 – When a lion or a bear came and carried off a sheep from the flock, I went after it, struck it and rescued the sheep from its mouth. When it turned on me, I seized it by its hair, struck it and killed it.

[10] 1 Peter 2:25

[11] Psalm 23:2

[12] Acts 20:29b-31a – Savage wolves will come in among you and will not spare the flock. Even from your own number men will arise and distort the truth in order to draw away disciples after them. So be on your guard!

[13] Exodus 14:14a – The Lord will fight for you.

[14] John 10:28 – I give them eternal life, and they shall never perish; no one can snatch them out of my hand.

[15] Psalm 23:2-3a

[16] Psalm 34:18 – The LORD is close to the brokenhearted and saves those who are crushed in spirit.

[17] Psalm 147:3 – He heals the brokenhearted and binds up their wounds.

9

A Blessing From Heaven

"Beauty, sweet love,
is like the morning dew."
Samuel Daniel

"Joy descends gently upon us
like the evening dew,
and does not patter down like a hailstorm."
Jean Paul

*D*ew.
Do you ever think about dew? I doubt many of us do, unless perhaps we've been camping and have awakened with a moist sleeping bag and damp pajamas.

Dew is a remarkably predictable daily occurrence in our world. As the sun dips below the horizon, temperatures cool, and night quietly descends like a soft canopy, wrapping the earth in its tender embrace. The warm ground radiates heat into the air. As the night air begins to cool, it can no longer hold all the moisture; water vapor condenses out on the ground and the plants as dew gently and unpretentiously begins to form. The process continues all night long, covering the earth's surface with its abundant goodness.

We may not think much about dew, but life would be radically different without it. In arid areas where rainfall is scarce, dew is essential for watering vegetation; it even provides water for animals. It is life itself. As dew covers a plant, it absorbs the life-sustaining material through its foliage. Without dew, life in these parched lands would cease.

Scripture refers to dew quite often—35 times to be exact! Dew is seen as a blessing from God.[A] Before the flood, dew was likely the way God watered the earth. Just as dew is nature's way of providing for and renewing life on the face of the earth, spiritual dew is God's way of providing spiritual life—refreshment and renewal—for His people.

> "I will be like the dew to Israel;
> he will blossom like a lily."
> Hosea 14:5a

God is speaking to His people with a promise: He will be the spiritual dew for His people, to quietly nourish them so they "will blossom"[1]—flourish, thrive, and succeed! God speaks that same promise to us today! Yet sadly, because many Christians don't realize the importance of heavenly dew in their lives, they inadvertently interfere with this special blessing from God! As a result, they lack freshness and vitality; they droop from spiritual dryness.

How this works

Think of the dew in your backyard. At night when the leaves or flower petals are quiet and at rest, the pores open to collect the cool and nourishing bath. Dew forms in quiet when the air is calm, and the winds subside. In fact, it forms so silently and gradually that we don't notice it until it is already there. Dew doesn't call attention to itself the way rain does. It makes no demands. It humbly and faithfully shows up day after day as it gently nourishes the earth, then fades away as the day dawns in full.

Likewise, "spiritual dew," Author Lettie B. Cowman tells us, "comes from quiet lingering in the Master's presence."[B] Spiritual dew is God Himself covering His people with His blessings, favor, grace, and love—essentially His presence! Dew doesn't gather when there is a flurry of activity. Rushing around thwarts dew from covering us fully, if at all. The whirlwind of activity must stop.

It is only when we are still before the Lord—when we silence the cacophony of noise around us—that our spiritual pores can open to receive God's riches. As we seek Him in quiet reverence,[2] we anticipate His drenching.

God will be faithful! He will quietly cover us with His spiritual presence as His nourishing, generous love gently washes over us in our stillness. Physical dew is renewed day by day and God, in His extravagant grace, likewise grants us a fresh soaking of spiritual dew every day. New every morning!

> Because of the LORD's great love…
> his compassions…are new every morning.
> Lamentations 3:22-23a

Friends, may God saturate you with the precious dew of Heaven as you eagerly seek Him in the stillness, rejuvenating your parched hearts and reviving your dry souls with His unfailing and abundant love. It is only then we can reflect Christ and His lavish goodness and encourage weary soldiers of the Kingdom.

If we fail to drink in every heavenly drop of this subtle, unassuming blessing, we may, like the plants of arid and desert climates, never survive. Soak in some of the blessings of heavenly dew, below, written with you in mind!

Enjoy the drenching. (Emphasis of "dew" is mine.)

May God give you heaven's **dew** and earth's richness…
Genesis 27:28a

———

May the Lord bless his land with the precious **dew** from heaven above and with the deep waters that lie below.
Deuteronomy 33:13

———

Let him be drenched with the **dew** of heaven…
Daniel 4:15b

———

…like **dew** from the Lord,
like showers on the grass, which
do not wait for anyone or depend on man.
Micah 5:7b

———

…the heavens will drop their **dew**.
Zechariah 8:12b

May God bless you with His unfailing glory and remind you of His profound love—a love that has NOTHING to do with who you are, what you do, or how well you do what you do. His is a love that embraces you no matter what. Always. Let that sink in and penetrate your soul for eternity.

God absolutely adores you!

---

[1] Hosea 14:7
[2] Psalm 46:10 – Be still and know that I am God.

10

✦

Light Amid Darkness

It was deplorable! More than a bit unnerving. We were standing in a very deep stone pit—an underground prison of sorts—located under the house of Caiaphas, the high priest in Jerusalem. This was likely where Jesus spent the night before His crucifixion. It was dark, damp, and gloomy. Stone cold and very isolating. We all stood there motionless with a sense of crushing agony, as we considered Jesus's final hours.

His soul was grieved beyond comprehension. He was condemned to die an excruciating death: mentally, physically, emotionally, and spiritually. His eyes were dim with sorrow and anguish. Deserted by His closest friends, He waited in the darkest depths—soon to take on our sins: past, present, and future. The wrath of God was about to be poured out upon Him.

Because of us.

The pit contained no windows. There was a single bulb dimly illuminating the room for us; I can't imagine how dark it must have been over 2000 years ago with no electric bulbs hanging overhead. In Charles Spurgeon's book, *Morning by Morning*, editor and theologian Jim Reimann commented, "Most likely, Jesus was lowered into this cold, totally dark pit and held overnight, completely alone."[A] As our tour guide in Israel, Jim told us there were roaches and mice everywhere. Cold in winter—hot in summer. Jesus would have been chained to the wall—his body up in the air. Hands above His head—legs apart. They would have put salt and vinegar in his wounds from the flogging. He suffered alone. In complete solitude.

No means of escape. And actually, because of His enormous love for us, Jesus had no desire to escape. He could have summoned 10,000 angels if He chose to, but He didn't. He was resolute; He was going to see this through—the reason He came to Earth 33 years ago. This was the purpose of His life.

> For the joy set before him
> [Jesus] endured the cross,
> scorning its shame…
> Hebrews 12:2b (brackets mine)

Jesus awaited His execution in the most austere and harshest of places. What joy was *set before him* that would cause Him to endure the cross?

That joy was you…and me.

We were the joy that gave Him the mettle and resolve to endure and carry the cross to completion. His love for us gave Him the fortitude the task required.

What an amazing fulfillment of a prophetic psalm. As our group stood there silently contemplating the obvious, Jim read this psalm to us.

Psalm 88

Lord, you are the God who saves me;
day and night I cry out to you.
May my prayer come before you;
turn your ear to my cry.

I am overwhelmed with troubles
and my life draws near to death.
I am counted among those who go down to the pit;
I am like one without strength.

I am set apart with the dead,
like the slain who lie in the grave...
You have put me in the lowest pit,
in the darkest depths...

You have taken from me my closest friends
and have made me repulsive to them.
I am confined and cannot escape;
my eyes are dim with grief.

I call to you, Lord, every day;
I spread out my hands to you...
Why, Lord, do you reject me
and hide your face from me? ...

All day long they surround me like a flood;
they have completely engulfed me.
You have taken from me friend and neighbor—
darkness is my closest friend.

The instant Jim finished reading the psalm, the Muslim call to prayer was broadcast in the far reaches above (one of the five times it goes out each day). It is a penetrating, musical sound in a minor key. Eerie and ominous are the adjectives that came to mind as my family and I processed the irreverent interruption. Was the timing of this call to Muslim prayer a coincidence?

Not a chance.

Here we were, underground in the dark stony abyss, feeling a heavy aura of hopelessness. Yet we all came to a piercing realization as we listened to the mystical call intruding upon our presence. Despite being physically in the dark void, as Christ-followers, we were abiding in the light of life. Yet there were so many people above us—hundreds, perhaps thousands—answering that call to prayer. Despite standing in the bright sunlight, they were residing in total spiritual darkness.

Utterly spiritually lost.

What a curious irony.

Spiritual darkness

All people live in spiritual darkness at one point in their lives. This refers to living a life apart from the one true living God. Jesus invites us out of spiritual darkness—and into the light of His love. When we respond to Him and confess our faith in God, our eyes are opened. And the most remarkable transformation occurs! We become a new creation.[1] We turn from darkness to light—from the power of Satan to the power of God.[2] And we begin a personal relationship with Jesus Christ.

Make no mistake; we are either under the power of the Holy Spirit or under the power of Satan. There is no middle ground. We are set apart by our faith to become beacons of the spiritual light of Jesus[3] to the world. We will never walk in darkness again[4] but will *always* have the light of eternal life.[5]

No matter how dark our situation feels, it is only a mirage. We are residents of the eternal light of glory! Stay connected to the Holy Spirit; ask Him to fill you each day so your light never goes out.

In this world ruled by Satan, I expect there to be darkness. But what is most disturbing is the absence of light. Where are all the Christians? Dr. Tony Evans says, "The problem is we have Christians as dark as the world...

This is not a time for secret agent Christians. This is the time for Christians to go public."B

Embrace this light of Christ. Expect, however, that as we shine our light, we become a target for the enemy. Christian author and Bible teacher Jennifer Rothschild says, "Consider it a compliment and an honor when the enemy throws darts in your direction. He may rattle you, but he can't overcome you"C Your light threatens his darkness. Stand strong against his tricky tactics; he can't win. The indwelling Holy Spirit is far more powerful![6] The light of Jesus in you will always prevail over the enemy!

Walk in this light. Boldly and with courage, shine the light of His glory into the darkness of our world, not so that others can see you, but so they can see Jesus as you reflect His goodness, His Truth, and His love—to a world desperate for hope—the hope of Christ.

---

[1] 2 Corinthians 5:17, ESV – If anyone is in Christ, he is a new creation. The old has passed away; behold, the new has come.

[2] Acts 26:18a – Open their eyes and turn them from darkness to light, and from the power of Satan to God.

[3] Ephesians 5:8a – You were once darkness, but now you are light in the Lord.

[4] Colossians 1:13 – He has rescued us from the dominion of darkness and brought us into the kingdom of the Son he loves.

[5] John 8:12b – Whoever follows me will never walk in darkness, but will have the light of life.

[6] 1 John 4:4b – The one who is in you is greater than the one who is in the world.

11

Casualties Are Likely

recently bought a new car—a pre-owned Mini Cooper convertible. Caribbean blue. A 6-speed—even better! It's a playful car and just plain fun to drive! I drove a stick years ago. And I drove one again a few years ago when we were touring Luxembourg, soaking up my ancestral roots. We needed a rental car and found most cars in Europe have manual transmission. A car with automatic transmission would cost an *additional* $90/day above and beyond the rates for a stick—plus taxes! So, we rented one with a stick shift.

After many jolting fits and starts, we were off! What fun we had! This planted the idea deep within me that my next car had to be a 6-speed. Two years later, my dream came true!

One day I was running tight for an appointment. I zipped into the lot, quickly parked, and turned off the engine. Distracted, I opened the door to exit, only to find myself tripping as I tried to stand—the car was moving forward. I attempted to brace myself against the open door and hold the car back from rolling; this proved to be grossly ineffective. I had forgotten to engage the emergency brake. Thankfully, my car drifted into the curb.

As I pondered the disaster that could have happened, I considered the power of words. When we are distracted, words tend to escape our mouths with abandon, tripping us up as they tumble out—a cascade of words, one falling on top of another—before we realize it. We can try to stop the damage by attempting to fix the offense, but likely this will be grossly ineffective.

Don't you wish we had an emergency brake lever for our mouths? Oh, but we do! In essence, the Holy Spirit is our emergency brake.

Left to our own devices

Our mouths speak what is contained in our hearts.[1] As our words make the short journey from our hearts to our mouths, our emotions churn and swirl, getting our words all tangled up as they seek a quick exit. When we're distracted, we may not always be aware of what comes toppling out, uncensored and unabated. Before we know it, we realize the damage we've done, the person we've hurt, the harm we've inflicted. We may try to pull back our words or turn them around to lessen the damage…to little avail. It's so important to guard what's in our hearts. Like water overfilling a bucket, our words spill out as overflow.[2]

I remember one large senior high Sunday School class my husband and I taught. The students sat in a circle on the floor as we handed out paper plates and tubes of toothpaste. On cue, they squeezed the toothpaste out onto the paper plates. When satisfied their tubes were empty, we instructed them to put as much of the toothpaste back into the tubes as possible. Full of optimism and energy, using toothpicks, popsicle sticks, and Q-tips, they enthusiastically tried with all their might to force the paste back into their tubes. Minutes passed feverishly as their countenances sank with each failed attempt until, with slumped shoulders, they finally gave up—exasperated and defeated.

We calmly explained that this was an object lesson. The toothpaste represented our words which can spew out of our mouths recklessly, thoughtlessly—in a flash—without much effort. But they are impossible to put back in, no matter how hard we try, how long we work, or what tools we use.

What a powerful illustration of the necessity to speak carefully because we can't take our words back. Once out, words carry power—power to bless or power to hurt.

Much power for evil

Curiously, the Bible has a lot to say about the words that come out of our mouths.

> Words are powerful; take them seriously.
> Words can be your salvation.
> Words can also be your damnation.
> Matthew 12:37, MSG

James has the most well-known verses on the power of the tongue. He observes that large ships are steered by a very small rudder. Likewise, the tongue, so small, wields great power. It takes a small spark to set fire to a great forest. The tongue, like a fire, can unleash a world of evil with the power to possibly ruin a life. An uncontrolled tongue can do considerable damage.[3] It is filled with poison that can kill.[4] Consider these warnings:

> I killed you [your reputation, self-esteem, etc.]
> with the words of my mouth.
> Hosea 6:5b (brackets mine)

His mouth is full of lies and threats;
trouble and evil are under his tongue.
Psalm 10:7

———✿———

You use your mouth for evil
and harness your tongue to deceit.
Psalm 50:19

———✿———

They sharpen their tongues like swords
and aim cruel words like deadly arrows.
They shoot from ambush at the innocent;
they shoot suddenly, without fear.
Psalm 64:3-4

———✿———

The words of the reckless
pierce like swords.
Proverbs 12:18a

———✿———

A perverse tongue
crushes the spirit.
Proverbs 15:4b

———✿———

Their tongue is a deadly arrow;
it speaks deceitfully.
Jeremiah 9:8a

We dare not be careless with our words. Though we may apologize, the pain has been inflicted. The damage our remarks cause can last years or a lifetime. A few reckless words can destroy a lifelong friendship. They can ruin reputations and hurt our integrity.

Equal power for good

Despite its power to harm, the tongue has incredible power to bless, heal, and restore. Consider these verses:

The tongue of the righteous is choice silver.
Proverbs 10:20a

———

The soothing tongue is a tree of life.
Proverbs 15:4a

———

The tongue has the power of life and death.
Proverbs 18:21a

———

Like apples of gold in settings of silver
is a word spoken at the right time.
Proverbs 25:11, AMP

———

Even fools are thought wise…if they hold their tongues.
Proverbs 17:28

———

Watch your tongue and keep your mouth shut,
and you will stay out of trouble.
Proverbs 21:23, NLT

———

Do you really love life? Do you want to be happy?
Then stop saying cruel things and quit telling lies.
1 Peter 3:10, CEV

Our words are a quick reflection of what is contained within our hearts. If what we're about to say doesn't bring glory to God, we must exercise self-control (a spiritual fruit)[5], engage the emergency brake, and keep silent. Otherwise, casualties are likely.

It came out of nowhere

My Mini Cooper. My dream car. I waited years to get it. Sadly, just a few months after I got it, a drenching rain pounded as I sat at a stop light. A large Jeep barreled into me at 45 mph, throwing me forward. My cherished car was totaled. The airbags didn't deploy; the seat belt didn't engage. I shouldn't have survived. But God... There is no explanation except to say God's ministering angels had some purpose in allowing me to walk away unharmed.

For the first many days, I was greatly saddened. I felt violated, my dream ripped from me after enjoying it for only a short time. But God...He opened my eyes to see that it's not about my dream or my comfort; it's about His glory.

Amidst this heartbreak, I choose gratitude. Gratitude that my life was spared. Gratitude that I enjoyed my dream car, even if for too short a time. Gratitude that this isn't about me. If it were, my story would have a sad, meaningless ending. But it's about God's glory. So, I choose to trust He has a greater purpose through this challenge that I cannot see. I rest in His sovereignty, knowing He will be glorified through this somehow. My purpose is to reflect His glory.

---

[1] Matthew 12:34b, NLT – Whatever is in your heart determines what you say.

[2] Proverbs 4:23 – Above all else, guard your heart, for everything you do flows from it.

[3] James 3:5-6 – The tongue is a small part of the body, but it makes great boasts. Consider what a great forest is set on fire by a small spark. The tongue is also a fire, a world of evil among the parts of the body. It corrupts the whole body, sets the whole course of one's life on fire, and is itself set on fire by hell.

[4] James 3:8b – [The tongue] is a restless evil, full of deadly poison.

[5] Galatians 5:22-23a, ESV – The fruit of the Spirit is...self-control.

12

The Miracle Mile

The excitement surrounding this race was palpable. Roger Bannister of England, a highly trained 25-year-old athlete, became the first man in the world to run a mile in under 4 minutes—3:59.4 to be exact—on May 6, 1954 in Oxford, England. But he only held the record for just over 6 weeks. On June 21st, John Landy of Australia took the title in Turku, Finland with a time of 3:58.[A]

It was decided that these two runners would face each other for the first time. And the world would be watching! On August 7, 1954, the two men met in the newly constructed Empire Stadium in Vancouver, Canada. The race received coverage in the world press with an estimated 100 million enthusiastic viewers across the American continent. Live radio coverage was provided to Australia and the rest of the world.[B] Promoted as *The Mile of the Century*, it would later be referred to as *The Miracle Mile*.[A]

A little-known fact is that both runners had health issues that day. Bannister was battling a cold with a bad cough; Landy had a deep, 1.6-inch long gash on the instep of his left foot which sported four stitches.[B]

The highly anticipated race was soon to begin. As 35,000 enthusiastic fans packed the stadium and took their seats, both men approached the starting blocks. The world eagerly tuned in. And one of the most memorable races in history commenced with a fervor rarely seen. It was a tight race. With just 90 yards to go, John Landy was in the lead. But he then did something he would live to regret; he glanced over his left shoulder to check Bannister's position, a mistake that slowed his pace ever so slightly. Roger Bannister noticed and took advantage by streaking past him to take the win with a time of 3:58.8. Landy finished just 0.8 seconds behind him.[B] This was the first time the four-minute mile had been broken by two men in the same race.[A]

Running the spiritual race

What a powerful illustration of the spiritual race we are all running. We seem to start off well, running in our individual lanes, but at some point we get distracted by looking from side to side into other people's lanes. We compare our run to those around us. Perhaps we engage with social media and see our friends living the "ideal" life. We become too preoccupied looking at everyone else's lanes that we lose our footing. We stumble while others gain ground. We judge ourselves harshly, telling ourselves we are too slow. Discouragement takes hold. And we fall behind.

God has given you a lane. Run your best race—one step, then the next, then the next. Don't be tempted to look left or right to gauge how others are doing; their performance has no bearing on your race. Unlike Bannister and Landy, you're not running against competitors. Your running talents, strengths, and advantages make you unique and valuable. You can't compare your race to that of another person. A wise person observed, "Everybody is a genius. But if you judge a fish by its ability to climb a tree, it will live its whole life believing that it is stupid." Although this quote is attributed to Albert Einstein, there is some debate.

When the race gets hard, don't drop out and sit on the sidelines. Life is not a spectator sport. Keep running, but pace yourself so you don't burn out. Stay focused. Keep your eyes on the finish line and on the One who waits for you on the other side.

> Let us run with endurance and active persistence
> the race that is set before us,
> [looking away from all that will distract us and]
> focusing our eyes on Jesus,
> who is the Author and Perfecter of faith.
> Hebrews 12:1b-2a, AMP

This is your destiny—your purpose—to run your race of faith for God's glory, using the talents and abilities He has given you. As the Holy Spirit provides the grace you need to finish with unwavering resolve, you will find you are tougher than you think.

In his bestseller, *Don't Waste Your Life*, Dr. John Piper gives us a poignant reminder,

> "Remember, you have one life.
> That's all.
> You were made for God.
> Don't waste it."[C]

This is your race—your time in the sun. Run with everything you've got. People are watching and cheering for you to finish strong. Stay faithful. The glory of your race shines for eternity, reflecting the One who designed you perfectly to run your specific race for reasons you will not fully comprehend until you cross over to eternity.

Fun facts

As of June 2022, 1755 athletes have broken the four-minute mile.[D] The current world record is held by Hicham El Guerrouj of Morocco. In 1999, at the age of 24, he ran the mile in 3:43.13.[E] His average speed was 16.1435 mph.

———

The "Miracle Mile" was immortalized the year it was run (1954) in the very first issue of a brand-new magazine: Sports Illustrated.[F] That issue hit the newsstands on August 16, 1954.

———

Roger Bannister went on to become a doctor, earning his medical degree from Oxford in 1963. He became a neurologist and wrote papers on the physiology of exercise, heat illness, and neurological issues. He was knighted by Queen Elizabeth II in 1975.[G] Sir Roger Bannister died on March 3, 2018 at the age of 88[H] after suffering from Parkinson's disease for seven years.[I]

John Landy became the governor of the Australian state of Victoria, representing British royalty in the state. He devoted his life to agricultural research. He died on February 24, 2022 at the age of 91[J] after a long battle, also with Parkinson's disease.[K]

13

Standing in the Gap

Early in their journey traversing the desert, the Israelites encountered their first real challenge. They crossed paths with the Amalekites, descendants of Amalek, the grandson of Esau.[1] Esau was the son of Isaac, a patriarch of Israel. The Amalekites were a hostile, nomadic tribe who made their living by raiding settlements they happened upon. They killed for pleasure and stole whatever they could manage.[A]

The Amalekites spotted the Israelites one day and attacked them without warning. They zeroed in on those who were weary and feeble, lagging behind.[2] This was the first battle the Jews had fought since leaving Egypt. The Amalekites were seasoned warriors; the Israelites were not. Their only real-life experience was making bricks for their slave masters in Egypt.

Moses sprang into action by ordering Joshua to organize a strong defense. Joshua and the army fought the Amalekites with all they had. Meanwhile, Moses went up on a hill to watch the battle alongside Aaron and Hur. In that culture, Jews raised their hands when they prayed. So as Moses watched the battle unfold, he stood with arms lifted up, the staff of God in his hands.[3] And Israel was winning!

When his arms fatigued, he dropped them at his side and a peculiar thing happened! The Jews began getting overpowered. When Moses raised his hands again, the

Israelites prevailed. Every time he lowered his hands, the Amalekites gained the advantage. Aaron and Hur seated Moses on a stone and they held his hands up, one on each side—for hours! Until they defeated the Amalekites.[4]

Moses immediately built an altar, calling it, "The Lord Gives Me Victory."[5] He gave God the glory for the shared conquest. All who were present saw Moses reflecting the glory of the win to the One worthy of the glory.

A dual battle

This was obviously a dual battle: physical and spiritual. Military might and spiritual stamina were both needed for the victory. As well as prayerful intercession on their behalf.

We, too, will face battles that will come upon us suddenly. The enemy likes to attack us at our weakest point, when we are weary and feeling vulnerable. We will be wise to remember the wisdom of Moses as he battled with:

- Spiritual power

   He lifted up his arms in prayer, the staff representing God's authority. He knew he needed the power of God in Heaven to accomplish this victory. God worked through Moses to empower Joshua and his army to overcome the Amalekites. Dr. Tony Evans says, "When you pray, you usher in spiritual solutions to the problems at hand."[B]

   Jesus, too, lifted up his arms to be victorious—on the cross. But unlike Moses, He couldn't share the burden; He carried the full weight of the battle Himself.

- Physical prowess

  Moses enlisted the skills of Joshua and the army. He stepped out in courageous faith with an actionable plan to battle evil, leaning on God's strength. He didn't sit back in fear or discouragement, waiting for God to do something. God often likes to work for the victory through us, enlisting our participation. Success shared with the Lord is especially sweet.

- Intercession

  Moses interceded by praying for Joshua and the army. Aaron and Hur interceded for Moses, giving him the strength to persevere. All three helped carry the burden[6] by stepping forward when it mattered.

  We are most like Christ when we intercede in prayer for our friends. Our prayers pierce the throne of grace and are infused with divine power. Intercession in any form is a display of our love for others.

When facing a challenge, we must avoid thinking we can just pray and do nothing else. Or assume all responsibility in our human strength without enlisting God. And we mustn't be too proud to ask our Christian family and friends to help us spiritually when the burden becomes heavy. Jesus and the Holy Spirit are always interceding on our behalf.[7,8] They make it possible for us to keep our hands raised as we battle in His strength for His glory. And remember: our blessings ahead will always surpass our battles behind.

Immediately after securing the victory, Moses erected an altar to give the glory to God. Moses claimed none of the credit for himself but fully acknowledged God's hand in it. By deflecting the credit, he reflected the glory back to God. Moses honored God well.

We are blessed to share victories with the Lord, but He deserves all the glory.

[1] Genesis 36:12

[2] Deuteronomy 25:17-18

[3] This was a simple shepherd's staff, sanctified by God. Moses used it before to perform miracles in Egypt, trying to convince the Pharaoh to let his people go.

[4] Exodus 17:10-12

[5] Exodus 17:15, CEV

[6] Galatians 6:2 – Carry each other's burdens, and in this way you will fulfill the law of Christ.

[7] Romans 8:16b, ESV – We do not know what to pray for as we ought, but the Spirit himself intercedes for us with groanings too deep for words.

[8] Hebrews 7:25b – ...who [Jesus] always lives to intercede for them [those who come to God through him]. (Brackets mine.)

14

A Sacred Passage

It has been a tough season. Just after Christmas, my father-in-law died unexpectedly, leaving behind his wife with severe dementia. They were supposed to move across the country from Arizona to North Carolina (he was to live with us). After a year of planning, preparations were complete. Medical records had been transferred. Doctor appointments were on the calendar. Their rooms were ready. But it never came to pass. And since then, our family has suffered numerous other losses. All we know is we are left with a sizable hole in our hearts every single time.

I helplessly watch my friends cope with the emotional weight left behind as they deal with substantial losses. Far too many friends have lost young adult children. Others have buried husbands, wives, siblings, best friends, and parents way too young. They struggle to cope and find a new normal, which will never feel normal.

Death. It is repulsive to us. It feels so wrong—because it is! It wasn't supposed to be this way. Death wasn't part of creation, nor our original design. It runs counter to God's design for life. Yet, death is now inevitable because it is the wretched result of the fall of mankind.

When we lose someone close to us, a large part of us dies with our loved one, leaving behind a considerable void. The Earth pivots on its axis. Nothing is as it was.

"There are losses that rearrange the world.
Deaths that change the way you see everything,
grief that tears everything down.
Pain that transports you
to an entirely different universe,
even while everyone else
thinks nothing has really changed."[A]
Megan Devine
Grief consultant and author

In *A Grief Observed*, C.S. Lewis compared the death of a beloved to an amputation. "He will probably have recurrent pains in the stump all his life...He will always be a one-legged man. There will be hardly any moment when he forgets it."[B] Loss becomes a part of us as it integrates into our soul. It's not something we simply "get over."

Steve Leder, an American rabbi, pulls families aside at graveside services and says this, "There is nothing I can say to make this easier. Death is an awful part of life. This is one of those times when you just put one foot in front of the other until it's over. Just keep going. That is all you can do and that is all you must do. Put one foot in front of the other until today is over." If the response is, "I just can't," he replies, "You can and you will, because you must."[C]

Grief gains access to our heart the minute we give our heart to someone else. Grief is the loneliest journey we'll ever make. The pain of loss is so pervasive there is nothing it doesn't touch. What makes grief especially challenging is that every journey through it is unique. No two are alike which makes the grieving process a solitary one—a sacred journey we must traverse alone. No other person can fully identify with what we are feeling.

The presence of grief means we have loved. The depth of our grief reflects the relationship we shared and the intensity of our love. The more we love, the more we grieve; it's the price we pay for loving another. Yet we wouldn't choose to erase our pain by never having experienced the love we did.

> "Grief is like a long valley, a winding valley
> where any bend may reveal
> a totally new landscape."[D]
> C.S. Lewis

Grief is an endless journey with no finish line, no medal of achievement, and no blue ribbon awarded for making it through the pain. We simply must push through the best we can.

> "I thought I could describe a state;
> make a map of sorrow.
> Sorrow, however, turns out
> to be not a state but a process."[E]
> C.S. Lewis

Out of love, we carry the pain of loss so our loved one can be free; it's the cost of love—the final gift we can give them. We bear the burden and find our love is much stronger than our pain.

Jesus understands grief

Jesus stood beside a tomb and wept at the death of his dear friend. And in the wake of His tears, we find permission to cry our own. Not a single precious tear we shed goes unnoticed.[1] Voltaire reasoned, "Tears are the silent language of grief."

In our sorrow, when our hearts are broken and our spirits are crushed, God understands every emotion we experience. He balances our feelings of devastation and loss with the comfort of His presence, His love, and His abiding peace.

> The LORD is close to the brokenhearted;
> he rescues those whose spirits are crushed.
> Psalm 34:18

And yet...

We will have difficult days. Grief doesn't follow a clear, predictable progression through well-ordered stages. It often arrives without warning. Small things can trigger a fresh wave of grief: a simple song, a smell, or a sight. Within seconds, we are hurled into a time machine, transported back to "that moment." Time stands still as the world crashes at our feet and a profound emptiness washes over us.

Grief is Like Surfing

Grief is like surfing.
Except you're blindfolded.

In a hurricane.
And your surfboard is on fire.

And the people on the shore are shouting
surfing strategies for a storm they've never surfed.

And then shaking their heads
at how you handle the waves.[F]

Nicole Langman

Other times, grief lurks in the shadows like a dull, throbbing headache. It's exhausting. Grief is where love lingers, searching for a home.

Coping

As we walk through the valley, we gradually, painfully relinquish our old normal for a new normal. The old normal, which included our loved one will not return. It's only when we begin to embrace the new normal that we are able to move forward. The pain will always be there, but with God's help and guidance, we will be able to return to a full and meaningful life.

Gabby Jimenez, an end-of-life doula with The Hospice Heart, penned these words:

> "Grief is like a pair of muddy boots.
> The muddier they become,
> the harder it is to walk.
> That is what grief feels like.
> Grief is messy.
>
> Grief can be sticky and uncomfortable,
> and it can weigh so much
> that you feel like you are falling over
> a little bit each day
> from the weight of it all...
>
> One day...you will be able
> to walk a little easier.
> The mud will eventually dry;
> it will still stay on the boots,
> but it won't weigh as much.
> But this will take time."[G]

Grief will not always be this hard. The pain will lessen; the tears will stop falling. Although grief will not end, time will soften our sorrow such that the memory of our loved one will become a gentle, unexpected friend. Laughter will return. And we will learn how to move forward through the grief—because we know we must. It's fruitless to hold on to what was and miss out on what will be.

> "Sometimes I think of grief as a stranger
> knocking at my door…and I still let it in.
> Sometimes it's like an old friend, has its own key,
> and lets itself in. Sometimes I stand
> at the door and whisper…'go away.'"[H]
> Gabby Jimenez

The other side of grief

As our journey carries us to the other side of grief, we realize that grief has given us two beautiful gifts. The first is a treasure trove of precious memories to cherish—sweet blessings, so tender and pure. As the Holy Spirit brings them to mind, we can smile again—and even laugh.

The second is the legacy left by our loved one. As we embrace it, we realize we can go on, though we will bear an ache the rest of our lives. But we must carry that legacy forward as we honor our loved one and how their love changed us, impacted us, and grew us.

We must continue living. A wise person once asserted, "I will learn to live in the sunshine of your life rather than the dark shadow of your death." We can choose to live as a spring of joy and gratitude because we had the privilege of loving them or as a fountain of bitterness and pain that they were taken from us too soon. How would your loved one want you to live the rest of your life?

Our hope

Loss is hard, but as Christians, we rest in God's promise to always be with us. Our approach to death and grief is different from that of nonbelievers. We know death is not the end, but a beautiful passage to eternity, where our real life begins. All the drama here on Earth isn't life; it's just the prelude to our real life when all things are made new.[2]

The Holy Spirit gives us the courage we need to endure as He carries us through our valley of grief. Theodore Roosevelt stated, "Courage is not having the strength to go on; it is going on when you don't have the strength." We are able to push through it because our strength isn't rooted in ourselves, but in Christ.[3] This supernatural strength to which we have access is stronger than the power of loss; this gives us reason to smile. We are confident in what lies ahead. The anticipation of that future joy fills our present sorrows with hope. We do not grieve like those who have no hope.[4]

"Hope is like a star—
not to be seen in the sunshine of prosperity,
and only to be discovered
in the night of adversity."
Charles H. Spurgeon

No one ceases to exist. All people experience eternal life somewhere, but Christians experience it in Paradise with Jesus and those who have gone on before. Although we mourn, we rejoice that our loved one is living restored and whole with complete joy. We can rest assured that one day we will join them and enjoy the holiness of Heaven together. Although our hearts grieve for today, our souls carry our confident hope in the promise of Paradise for eternity.

God, being able to see all of eternity, holds a perspective we will never have. Therefore, the psalmist can say, "Precious in the sight of the LORD is the death of his saints."[5] The journey of believers through death to eternity is indeed a good thing. In *Every Moment Holy*, Douglas McKelvey shares a poignant prayer:

> Grant us courage to shrink neither from the aches nor from the joys that love brings, for each, willingly received, will accomplish the good works you have appointed them to do. Therefore we praise you even for our sadness, knowing that the sorrows we steward in this life will in time be redeemed.[1]

You will get through this. God sees and hears you as you grieve; He will meet your needs as you draw near to Him. He will not only strengthen you and give you courage to persevere, but comfort and carry you through the valley; His grace will be sufficient.[6]

Take His hand and don't let go! Praise Him for the blessing of knowing a love so strong. Just because your loved one died doesn't mean your love died. Love is eternal. Death doesn't have the final word for believers. Because Christ defeated death,[7] the cross has the final word, carries the ultimate victory, and boasts the glory of God!

---

[1] Psalm 56:8, NLT – You keep track of all my sorrows. You have collected all my tears in your bottle. You have recorded each one in your book.

[2] Revelation 21:5a

[3] Philippians 4:13, NKJV – I can do all things through Christ who strengthens me.

[4] 1 Thessalonians 4:13

[5] Psalm 116:15, KJV

[6] 2 Corinthians 9:12a – He said, "My grace is sufficient for you."

[7] 1 Corinthians 15:26 – The last enemy to be destroyed is death.

15

～◌～

Healing the Heart

*L*ife is filled with loss—all kinds of loss. But perhaps the most painful loss is that of a loved one through death. If we choose to love, we will suffer grief. Grief is piercing; it causes acute and intense sorrow, sadness, and anguish. Jesus understands—and He meets us in the deep abyss of our profound anguish, extending hope that transcends the grave. Here are simple considerations that may be helpful, and even therapeutic, during grief.

• **REALIZE** that in the early stages, grief expresses itself in a very physical manner. You may have trouble thinking and remembering even the simplest things. You may overeat or undereat. Insomnia may haunt you or perhaps you will sleep all the time. You may experience anxiety and panic attacks. Grief may feel like fear. Seek medical help, if warranted, to help you cope and get through the long hours during this season.

• **MOURN**. Take time to reflect, recall memories, and look at pictures and other memorabilia. Thank God for the love you shared. Talk with those who knew your loved one. Fully engage with this painful new reality. Embrace it. Lean into it. Allow the tears to flow. It's part of the healing process. Jesus made us a promise:

"Blessed are those who mourn,
for they will be comforted."
Matthew 5:4

As we grieve, the fingers of God's grace transform our sorrow into hope—the absolute confidence we have in God's promise that future joy *will* find us again as we heal.[1]

• **IMMERSE** yourself in God's Word; it strengthens and encourages. Camp out in the Psalms.

My soul is weary with sorrow;
strengthen me according to your word.
Psalm 119:28

• **CONNECT** with friends. Although the desire to be alone can be strong, don't completely isolate yourself. Be around people who love you, ideally several times per week.

A sweet friendship
refreshes the soul.
Proverbs 27:9b, MSG

• **ENGAGE** with nature. Get outside and enjoy the intricacies of God's beautiful creation. Fresh air and exercise are therapeutic. Notice the colors of the foliage, shrubbery, and flowers. Listen for the rustling of leaves, the song of birds, the chatter of squirrels, the bark of dogs, and the scurrying of rabbits. Inhale the smell of fresh leaves, the fragrance of flower blossoms, the aroma of food grilling, the scent of freshly cut grass, or the whiff of a recent rainfall. All creation sings His praises and gives Him glory—treasures for us to discover.

You are worthy, our Lord and God to receive glory
and honor and power, for you created all things.
Revelation 4:11a

- **LISTEN** to hope-filled Christian music. Sing along if you can. Make music through your brokenness; it heals. Music is a form of worship.

Worship the Lord with gladness;
come before him with joyful songs.
Psalm 100:2

Move to the music. Dance with abandon and don't worry if anyone sees you! Start now. If you wait, you may miss the rainbow on the other side of the storm. Every week should be easier than the week before.

"Life isn't about waiting for the storm to pass.
It's about learning how to dance in the rain."[A]
Vivian Greene

While in the backyard with our dogs one evening, I started dancing in the grass. When I went in the house, our next-door neighbor texted me. He said, "Dance like no one's watching!" I broke out laughing!

- **SURRENDER** to God. Dr. Timothy Keller asserted, "Christian faith is not a negotiation, but a surrender. It means to take your hands off your life,"[B] trusting God to take control. No matter how much you lose in this world, you will never lose God. As you seek Him for guidance and support, your burdens will begin to ease. He sees your weariness and will provide what you need to journey through your grief. It is only with His power working through your weaknesses that you can rise above the pain as you praise Him in the midst of your loss. This is a sacrifice of praise[2]—praising when it's hard; and it lifts up a sweet fragrance to the heavens in glory to God. So let your praises roar to the heavens and watch hope rise from the embers of your misery. Your only opportunity to worship during your suffering is on this side of eternity. Worship opens the window of your soul to fully receive His comfort, compassion, and love.

When we lift our hands to Him in surrender and praise, watch the darkness flee as an inexplicable peace replaces fear and anxiety; joy will eventually follow.

> May my prayer be set before you like incense;
> may the lifting up of my hands
> be like the evening sacrifice.
> Psalm 141:2

When Dr. Timothy Keller was dying, he assured his family, "There is no downside for me leaving, not in the slightest."[C] In one of his sermons on death, he proclaimed, "All death can do to Christians is make their lives infinitely better."[D]

• **CONSIDER** a pet. Sometimes a new life in the home is exactly what you need. But don't buy one on impulse; caring for a pet is a big responsibility. Fully commit to loving and caring for it for life.

• **JOY** is not a betrayal. It's perfectly natural to feel that if you experience laughter or joy, you have betrayed the one you've lost. It's not a betrayal; joy is a reflection of healthy grief. Your loved one would be distressed beyond measure to see you stop living, choosing gloom and despair as your companions. Here's a startling paradox: sorrow and joy can and do coexist. They aren't opposites; they work together. You aren't finished living; live in a way that honors your loved one, glorifies God, and reflects His goodness.

Seek out movies, clips, images, or jokes you know will make you laugh. Laughter has many health benefits and can be a quick vacation from grief.

Even in laughter the heart may ache.
Proverbs 14:13a

- **ACKNOWLEDGE** the many feelings you'll experience on this journey. Feeling overwhelmed is common. You may feel you will not be able to make it without your loved one. You will. Grief is a waxing and waning process. It gets better one moment and worse the next. Feelings are unreliable. God understands your feelings. Every. Single. One. You can count on it!

Cast all your anxiety on him
because he cares for you.
1 Peter 5:7

God will meet all your needs.
Philippians 4:19a

- **IT'S OKAY** to admit you're not okay. Grief takes time. Lots of time. And it's different for each person. There is no "normal." Don't compare your grief journey with that of another. No matter how dark the night, the sun will rise again. You will be okay, just not now. And that's okay.

- **WRITE** in a journal. Expressing thoughts on paper (or on the computer) can be restorative.

- **SERVE** others. Many people are hurting in a great variety of ways. Helping others strengthens us, eases our pain, and anoints our spirit with blessings that restore our purpose.

- **DO NOT EMBRACE** your grief as your new identity. In their book, *Grieving with Hope: Finding Comfort as you Journey through Loss*, authors Hodges and Leonard state, "Grief is a profound experience to go through, and it rocks a person at the core. It's disruptive, dislocating, and highly emotional. But this experience doesn't define me. Christ defines me."[E] You are a child of God in the midst of your grief. You are NOT your grief.

- **JOIN** a grief support group. Grief Share is exceptional. (griefshare.org) It is a Christ-centered, nondenominational grief recovery support group ministry that has helped scores of people work through their grief. They offer many class options.

    It is designed to extend support through the long months after the death, when people around the griever have returned to their normal busy lives. They also offer daily email encouragements for those who sign up online.

Your journey through grief may be the most difficult challenge you've ever faced. As you traverse this valley of sorrow with God, allow Him to carry and sustain you. One day you'll realize the comfort He offers and the peace He pours out on you are truly enough.

Even though I walk through the valley
of the shadow of death,
I will fear no evil, for you are with me;
your rod and your staff, they comfort me.
Psalm 23:4, ESV

You will never completely travel to the end of your grief. But it changes with time and does get easier. It's a passage, not a place to stay. The secret is to keep moving forward. Don't set up camp in the valley of despair. You aren't staying there; you're passing through. You will learn to rebuild around the loss. You will be whole once more, although not quite the same. Your life will again hold meaning. You are forever changed, immeasurably enriched by the priceless love you shared with the one you lost.

> They live forever in your broken heart that doesn't seal back up. And you come through. It's like having a broken leg that never heals perfectly—that still hurts when the weather gets cold, but you learn to dance with the limp.[F]
> Anne Lamott

And as you limp through life, you'll always remember, with a smile, the pure joy you carry because of the impact your loved one had on you. And one day, you will join them in Paradise. When the apostle John struggled to describe Paradise, he felt the best way was to contrast it with what we are familiar with.

He will wipe every tear from their eyes. There will be no
more death or mourning or crying or pain.
Revelation 21:4a

When Christian singer Steven Curtis Chapman lost his 5-year-old daughter to a fatal accident, Pastor Greg Laurie offered a beacon of hope during his darkest hour: "I want to encourage you that Maria is in a much greater part of your future than she is in your past." Our hope is not in this life, but in the life to come: Heaven.

May the promise of Heaven encourage and sustain you, as it has done for millions of people throughout history. Heaven—the place we will dwell in the glory of God for eternity—with Him and those we have loved.

Ahhhh…Paradise indeed!

---

[1] Psalm 126:5, NKJV – Those who sow in tears shall reap in joy.
[2] Hebrews 13:15 –Through Jesus, therefore, let us continually offer to God a sacrifice of praise—the fruit of lips that confess his name.

16

Finding Calm Amid Chaos

*I*t all happened one day on the Sea of Galilee. Nestled nearly 700 feet below sea level, the Sea of Galilee is like a bowl of water thirteen miles long, seven miles wide, and about 150 feet deep. It is mostly surrounded by mountains.

One evening, bone weary after a full day of teaching on the shore of the Sea of Galilee, Jesus suggested to his disciples, "Let us go over to the other side."[1] The disciples enthusiastically clamored into the boat with Jesus. Looking forward to relaxing at the end of their hectic day, they left the crowds behind, as waves gently lapped at the sides of their craft.

The Jesus Boat

Let's take a few minutes and consider what the fishing boats looked like in biblical times.

In the winter of 1986, a terrible drought gripped Israel; the Sea of Galilee had receded significantly. Two fishermen, brothers Moshe and Yuval Lufan, frequently walked along the shore looking for artifacts. As amateur archaeologists, it had always been their hope to discover a boat in the Sea of Galilee.

One day, they were startled to stumble upon just that— a boat encased in the mud along one edge. After careful digging, they uncovered one of the greatest archaeological finds in the history of Israel: an archaic, intact fishing boat—the same kind Jesus and his disciples would have used.[A] In fact, radiocarbon dating revealed this wooden boat was used sometime between 40 B.C. and A.D. 50, around the time Jesus lived.[B] Its construction was typical of ancient boats in the Mediterranean region of that time.[C]

A great excavation ensued. Top archaeologists got to work. On the first day, a sudden, heavy downpour, lasting only one minute, created a perfect double rainbow across the Sea of Galilee. An excavator observed this as God's blessing upon their discovery.[D]

After an 11-day dig, with researchers working around the clock, the boat was fully uncovered; it was 27 feet long, 7.5 feet wide, and 4.3 feet high.[C] This would have been big enough to hold Jesus and His disciples, but not much more.

This boat was found in the area of Gennesaret, where Jesus and His disciples landed after Jesus walked on the waters of the Sea of Galilee.[D]

bb

Archaeologists called this boat, *The Jesus Boat*. Today it is beautifully displayed in the Yigal Allon Galilee Boat Museum on the shore of the Sea of Galilee.

Back to the boat ride

It was calm as Jesus and His disciples set out that evening, but during their journey, a massive storm broke out without warning! Surrounded by mountains, the Sea of Galilee has always been prone to sudden storms. Cool Mediterranean air from the mountains descends quickly through the valleys, generating winds that funnel through narrow gorges and collide with the warm, moist air over the sea. Within minutes, these contrasting air masses can churn the water into violent waves several feet high. Boats caught out at sea during a sudden storm are in imminent danger.

In describing the windstorm, Mark referred to it as a furious squall or hurricane. The Greek word Matthew used was *seismos*, meaning "like an earthquake."[1] This word was also used:

- At Jesus's death when He defeated sin on the cross.[2]
- At Jesus's resurrection as He rose victorious over sin.[3]

This was one powerful storm! Imagine what it would have felt like in such a long narrow boat! As you can imagine, their craft quickly filled with water. At least four of the disciples were experienced fishermen: Andrew, Peter, James, and John. They spent their lives on the Sea of Galilee. These men knew how to handle a boat; they had a deep respect for the sea and the power of the water.

The storm raged. Jesus, exhausted from teaching all day, slept on a cushion in the rear of the boat as the waves crashed over the hull.

Even though the men were experienced sailors, they panicked, consumed with fear. Jesus had just healed a leper, a paralyzed man, Peter's mother-in-law, and many others.

He cast out demons, provided a miraculous catch of fish, restored sight and hearing, healed a shriveled hand, and raised a widow's only son from the tomb! Despite having just seen Jesus perform numerous incredible miracles, faith evaporated.

Awakened by the disciples, Jesus rebuked the wind the same way a parent would rebuke a misbehaving child. Imagine the faces of His disciples when the wind immediately obeyed Jesus! After gaping in awe at the suddenly calm sea, their gaze turned to Jesus in reverent wonder. They realized they were in the presence of a person mightier than the fury of a stormy sea. With eyes wide, trembling, they haltingly asked, "What kind of man is this?"[4] They struggled to fathom that Jesus, their friend, was the God of the universe and in control of the wind and waves.

As they fixed their gaze on Jesus, The King James Bible says "they feared exceedingly."[5] Their fear took a critical turn at this juncture. Debilitating (self-focused) fear of the storm transitioned to a reverent (Christ-centered) fear (awe) of God. Jesus replaced their unhealthy fear with a healthy fear.

> The fear of the LORD leads to life.
> Proverbs 19:23a

Storms will come

We will have no shortage of storms in our lives which can descend upon us without warning. Until they hit, we deceive ourselves into thinking we have life under control—until we don't. Fear turns us into control freaks. "Someone needs to do something!" We fear what we cannot control.

Sometimes getting on board with Jesus pushes us into deep and turbulent waters. We can find ourselves in the middle of God's perfect will and in the center of a perfect storm at the same time! Just like the disciples.

With the storm at its peak, the disciples awoke Jesus. They didn't say, "Hey Jesus, are you aware of this storm?" or "Jesus, do you have experience with bad storms?" Instead, they raised doubts about His character. "Don't you care if we drown?"[6] Fear erodes our confidence in God's goodness. We may think, "A good God wouldn't let this happen."

Jesus allowed the wind to rage so His disciples would learn to trust Him. At times He does the same with us. Storms remind us of our own helplessness; we need Jesus. He wants us to come to Him with our fears. He yearns to show us how to exchange our worldly fears (which are destructive) for divine fear (which is healthy and necessary).

Storms will find us; we don't get to decide whether the rain is coming. When large pillows of stormy clouds roll in, blotting out the blue sky overhead, we will face a choice. We can stay ashore in hopes of avoiding the storm or step into the boat with Jesus. During a sermon, Dr. Stephen Rummage advised, "When you're in a storm, don't focus on how to get out of the storm. Focus on how to get Jesus into the boat. When Jesus is in the boat, you will arrive safely where you need to be. When Jesus gets on board, He doesn't get on board as a passenger or a crew member. He always gets on as captain and He'll take the boat where it needs to go. Jesus ultimately saves us from the storm."[F] When at the mercy of the tempest, being with Jesus is the safest place to be.

Be aware of your focus

- Your focus reveals your faith.
  It's either your guiding light or a distant flicker.
- Your focus determines your peace.
  Whatever you focus on will be magnified. If you allow yourself to be continually inundated with newsbites, don't be surprised when your anxiety and depression escalate and intensify. If you focus on Christ, trust grows, which fuels a sense of peace.

Our heavenly Father is kind and patient when the storms of life overwhelm us, the waves sweep over us, and anxiety grips us. Our cries may be riddled with fear and doubt. We feel so alone, but we aren't. Jesus told His disciples not to fear the storms that would inevitably crash over them. He tells us the same thing.

Will you listen?

(Please read the complete story in Mark 4:1, 35-41.)

---

[1] Mark 4:35b

[2] Matthew 27:50-52b – When Jesus had cried out again in a loud voice, he gave up his spirit. At that moment, the curtain of the temple was torn in two from top to bottom. The earth shook, the rocks split, and the tombs broke open.

[3] Matthew 28:2 – There was a violent earthquake, for an angel of the Lord came down from heaven and, going to the tomb, rolled back the stone and sat on it.

[4] Matthew 8:27b

[5] Mark 4:41a, KJV

[6] Mark 4:38b

17

Surviving the Desert

As I make my way across the hot, barren desert of my circumstances, I realize how desperate my situation has become. The brisk, mournful wind howls relentlessly across the wasteland of my soul.

All memories of fragrant flowers, vibrant flora, cheerful chatter of birds, and shimmering streams are forgotten. Only a bleak and inhospitable landscape remains. The relentless sun scorches the lifeless sand in all directions. The desolate panorama offers neither promise, nor hope. Just a dismal reminder remains of the sweltering, grim state of my situation.

> I am like a desert owl,
> like an owl among the ruins.
> Psalm 102:6

Are you in the middle of a desert, wandering alone in solitude? Do ruins lie all around, threatening to engulf you? Does it seem endless?

A place of preparation

The desert is a valuable place of preparation. Jesus began His earthly ministry in the desert for 40 days where He endured intense battles with the enemy. We too will spend time in the metaphorical desert as God prepares us for ministry.

> It has been granted to you on behalf of Christ
> not only to believe in him, but also to suffer for him.
> Philippians 1:29

God groomed Moses in the desert for four decades of powerful leadership. John the Baptist preached from the desert as He prepared the world for the Messiah. Elijah fled to the desert where God comforted and sustained this great prophet.

It is in the desert where God refines our strengths and talents so He can use them later for His glory. As God grows and shapes our character, He transforms us. The more we embrace our suffering, the more we look like Christ.

Pastor John Bevere states the wilderness is "a time of preparation for [our] destiny in God." For the last four years of her life, Ruth Graham suffered severe back pain from degeneration of her spine. She was bedridden, frail, and very weak. Yet she remained upbeat and thankful. On her bedroom wall hung a crown of thorns, given to Ruth and Billy by the mayor of Jerusalem years earlier. She gazed at that crown of thorns often, remarking, "Christ suffered for me far more than I ever will for Him. How can I complain?"[A]

A place of suffering

The desert is a powerful place—a place where we learn what our faith is made of. All our shortcomings become crystal clear, and our faith either grows or dwindles in the desert. God's ultimate purpose in the desert, however, is not the release from the pain of suffering.

If we could see the end from the beginning, our confidence in God would soar. Our courage would skyrocket. Our stamina would swell. It would make all the difference. We must trust that God's ultimate agenda is for our best and for His glory.

Suffering has the potential to increase our faith and mold our character in ways a life of ease cannot. It grows us to look more like Jesus. Trials can be His greatest means of building faith-filled disciples. It is through hardship that we learn God can be trusted to carry our burden as we hold to His promises. It is through pain that we find God is our comfort. It is through adversity that we realize God's enduring presence never fails.

Pastor Phillips Brooks advised, "Do not pray for easy lives. Pray to be stronger men." Ask God to reveal His purposes and grant hope in your wilderness wandering. Trust Him in the journey and look for ways to glorify Him in the desert. Some paths in life require our footsteps alone. Although it is a place of isolation where life is stripped of distractions, we aren't really alone in deserts as God dwells with us there. Look for Him. Sometimes it takes the solitude of the desert for us to see and hear the Lord.

A place of testing

In your weak moments, the enemy will try to drive you to the depths of despair where darkness prevails. Nevertheless, even in the deepest pit, His light will penetrate to the very core of your misery. Rise up! Trust God, pour into His Word, and pray. Ask Him to reveal Himself to you in ways you've never seen before.

Look around; notice others struggling to push up through hard places. Encourage and help one another as you reflect His glory!

A place of deliverance

The Israelites well knew the kind of arid and aimless ambling that occurs in the desert; God liberated them from slavery in Egypt to the desert—and through the desert to their Promised Land. Many years later, He led them from captivity in Babylon to their homeland of Jerusalem by way of a desert.

During this journey, the Lord went before them, as He does with us. "I will make a way in the wilderness."[1] It was a tough road for them; it may not be an easy passage for us either. As we traverse the inhospitable environment, we thirst for Him with all our heart and soul, knowing He is our Living Water in a harsh and desiccated land.

> Earnestly I seek you; I thirst for you,
> my whole being longs for you,
> in a dry and parched land
> where there is no water.
> Psalm 63:1

When we trust God, He rewards our faithfulness as He carries us through the harsh wilderness to an oasis of abundance on the other side. We know, as we press on across the sandy dunes at the end of our endurance, we will come to a spring of life-giving water—blessings in our journey—refreshment within our pockets of despair or discouragement. We need only to lift our eyes to notice His presence.

I will make rivers flow on barren heights,
and springs within the valleys.
I will turn the desert into pools of water,
and the parched ground into springs.
Isaiah 41:18

What comprises the barrenness of your soul? The desolation of busyness? The striving for recognition and acceptance? Of proving yourself? Pursuing financial success? Or material gain? It is all worthless—hollow. Yet, God is there and offers His unlimited power and everything needed to endure.

The wilderness isn't what it seems. This world isn't all there is. It is but a shadow of the greater reality. Don't let the desert defeat you; compared to eternity, it is short-lived. Embrace the journey. And trust God, no matter how bleak the days and sleepless the nights. He is always working in the background, doing things in your life you'd never believe—far more than you could possibly realize![2]

Perhaps your world is dark right now because God is unveiling some aspect of His glory too holy for you to see face to face. Praise Him—even in the gloomiest of days—for the privilege of having our hearts anchored in the eternal joys set before us.

Deserts don't last forever. Some deserts release us after a time; we don't emerge the same as we entered. God transforms souls in the desert, and He gives us gifts to ponder, treasure, and share with others as we journey on. Other deserts take us all the way to our eternal home, our land of promise where cool, flowing springs of Living Water are abundant.

Our faith has matured. We have grown in holiness.

For His glory.

---

1 Isaiah 43:19 – I am doing a new thing...I am making a way in the wilderness and streams in the wasteland.
2 Habakkuk 1:5, NLT – I am doing something...you wouldn't believe even if someone told you about it.

18

Rivets of Steel

It was April 14, 1912.

The fateful day of the deadliest sinking of a single ship up to that point in history. When the Titanic went down, more than 1500 people died.[A]

The Titanic, the largest and most luxurious ocean liner in the world at the time, was as tall as a 17-story building![B] It was the pinnacle of opulence with seven decks, squash courts, a Turkish bath, and a gym.[C] It also held two libraries, two barber shops, a heated swimming pool, swanky restaurants, and lavish cabins. It was one of the first ships with a telephone system and electric lights in all the rooms.[B]

The Titanic was dubbed "unsinkable" by the press[D] as it had, at that time, the most technologically advanced safety features designed to keep the ship afloat if damaged.[E] Only four days into her maiden voyage from Southampton, England to New York City, United States, the Titanic was cruising under mostly clear skies, the weather unremarkable.[F] Carrying 2223 passengers,[G] the Titanic struck an iceberg near Newfoundland at 11:40pm,[H] which tore into the starboard side, severing the hull and six of the sixteen watertight compartments designed to keep it afloat.[I] The ship then ripped in half and sank 2.4 miles[J] to the floor of the North Atlantic Ocean at 2:20am on the 15th. The 28°F icy waters sealed its fate. (28°F is the point below which salt water freezes.)[F]

Many years later, Jennifer Hooper McCarty, a materials scientist at Oregon Health and Science University, and Tim Foecke, a scientist at the National Institute of Standards and Technology studied the ship to figure out what made it break in half on impact. Their findings were shocking!

While constructing the Titanic, the shipbuilder was simultaneously tasked with manufacturing the Titanic's two large sister ships, putting a significant strain on the shipyard. Because of time constraints, the builders compromised on the quality of rivets that secured the steel hull plates. The Titanic contained more than 3 million rivets. Although they used steel rivets for the center of the ship, they settled for substandard, iron rivets in the bow and stern. These rivets contained high concentrations of slag, a residue that can weaken metal.[A]

When the Titanic hit the iceberg, McCarty and Foecke concluded through their investigation that the weaker iron rivets popped their heads, breaking on impact so the ship couldn't withstand the stress of a collision.[A] Compromise led to a tragic and fatal catastrophe.

A collision is inevitable

As we cruise through life with unremarkable days and calm skies, there will come a time when we collide with a spiritual iceberg. It's inevitable. The fate of the impact will depend upon the strength of the rivets of our faith holding us together.

When we are forced to endure dark hours of pain and sorrow—on our knees, crying out to God, as the frigid waves pound against our hull—we will know if our faith is strong enough to sustain us. Hard times reveal our beliefs. If we are being held together with a faith strong as steel, we will weather the impact well. If our rivets of faith are weak, the jolt will tear us apart and we will sink. Do we have what it will take to withstand the true challenges of life?

The time to strengthen the rivets of our faith is when the waters are calm, not in the middle of a storm. We can only strengthen our faith one way—with purposeful intention.

What is faith?

The writer of Hebrews tells us faith is knowing for certain something is true, even when we can't see it.[1] Augustine summarized it well: "Faith is to believe what we do not see, and the reward of this faith is to see what we believe." It is knowing God can be fully trusted. We display our faith as we rely, not on ourselves, but on God.

> "The greatest act of faith takes place
> when a man finally decides
> that he is not God."
> Johann Wolfgang von Goethe

Rabindranath Tagore, an Indian Christian poet, quipped, "Faith is the bird that feels the light and sings when the dawn is still dark."

What about those icebergs?

God knew we would face many spiritual icebergs in our lives, so He tells us how to prepare.

1. We must be certain the object of our faith is God.

> Be sure that your faith
> is in God alone.
> James 1:6a

2. We must know our convictions: the firmly held, deep-seated beliefs that make up our faith—but taken a step further. They are the rivets of our faith and guide our lives. They are not instincts, feelings, emotions, intuition, or impulses.

   Dr. Howard Hendricks makes this distinction: "A belief is something you will argue about. A conviction is something you will die for." We must make sure our convictions align with the heart of Christ. Our lives reveal our true convictions and thus our faith. It's impossible to live in contradiction to them. We must never compromise our convictions.

   We don't tolerate sin or actions that violate our convictions of faith. They lead us to repentance and the desire for holiness—to stand against sin without apology. Apologist G.K. Chesterton explained, "Tolerance is the virtue of the man without convictions." It's wise to examine the things we tolerate; they reveal the strength of our convictions.

3. We must not settle for weak faith.[2] It takes hard work to strengthen the rivets of our faith. We do so by being in God's Word daily, studying scripture, praying, worshipping regularly, learning from the insight of biblical teachers and scholars, and fostering healthy Christian relationships.

Even when...

our faith is solid and the crisis hits, it is normal to feel fear, but it won't paralyze us for long. Max Lucado asserts, "Feed your faith and your fears will [starve]." As we confidently raise our shield of faith[3] and battle in Jesus's strength,[4] keeping our eyes on Him,[5] we will come out on top. Our faith will equip us to handle challenges with courage as we trust God through them.

Our faith is the victory that overcomes the world.
1 John 5:4, ESV

Another consideration

Inaction and silence are powerful reflections of the content of our heart. Here are two powerful quotes by Rev. Martin Luther King, Jr.

"Our lives begin to end the day
we become silent about things that matter."

—⁓—

"A man dies when he refuses to
stand up for that which is right.
A man dies when he refuses to
stand up for justice.
A man dies when he refuses to
take a stand for that which is true."

Let's muster the courage and confidence needed to stand against injustice, immorality, and evil—the very things that break the heart of God. Dietrich Bonhoeffer, a German theologian executed in 1945 by the Nazis, maintained,

"Silence in the face of evil is itself evil;
God will not hold us guiltless.
Not to speak is to speak.
Not to act is to act."

Convictions, if real, will move us to action. How strong are your convictions? Enough to die for?

A spiritual collision is inescapable

Can your convictions withstand the impact of the next collision? Are you prepared to handle it with rivets of faith as strong as steel? One day, everything will make perfect sense when our faith becomes sight—why we faced so many challenges: our pain and suffering, prejudice, difficult people, persecution, fears, and anxieties. And we will be forever glad we held strong to convictions of steel.

Until that day, faith is praising God in the crisis, trusting Him in the chaos, following Him in the darkness, and testifying to His glory.

You glorify God when you refuse to compromise your convictions of faith. These "rivets" will uphold you and lead you to victory of the soul. And as you reflect the hope of your faith by your actions and words, those who are struggling against the dark, icy waters will see you. As their world sinks into turmoil, they may reach out in desperation to grab hold of what is sustaining you.

Your life makes a radical difference!

Praise God!

---

[1] Hebrews 11:1, TLB – Faith is…the certainty that what we hope for is waiting for us, even though we cannot see it.

[2] 1 Peter 5:9

[3] Ephesians 6:16 – Take up the shield of faith.

[4] Philippians 4:13, ESV – I can do all things through him who strengthens me.

[5] Hebrews 12:2 – …fixing our eyes on Jesus.

19

Heavenly Citizenship

You've seen them—those little apartments built above stores. You can run a store or business downstairs and live upstairs. Pretty cool commute: you spend zilch on gas!

What a great illustration depicting the Christian life! Although we temporarily live down here on Earth, we're not really citizens down here. The Bible tells us, "Our citizenship is in heaven."[1] We're supposed to work and interact with people down here, but we live (in our spirit) up there! Never lose sight of this truth.

As citizens of Heaven, we must keep our focus on what's going on in the heavenlies as we work, serve, have fun, and interact with people down here.

Down here, however, is a problem because we live in a corrupt, fallen world controlled by Satan. And that will *always* be a problem!

Don't be tricked into thinking we live, work, and function on Earth, independently of what's going on in the spiritual realm. Satan will try to snow you. Down here isn't all there is. There is so much going on—up there!

As Christians, how should we live?

Engaging with the world requires steering clear of materialistic values or we may find ourselves sliding down the slippery slope to places we don't want to go!

1) We shouldn't isolate ourselves from the world, but go into the world, serving and making disciples. However, we must do so with discretion, as the world, controlled by Satan, is at odds with God.

> Go and make disciples of all nations.
> Matthew 28:19a

2) If we aren't careful, we may develop friendship with the world, which puts us in a dangerous position.

> Anyone who chooses to be a friend
> of the world becomes an enemy of God.
> James 4:4b

3) As friends of the world, we then slowly conform to the world's value system, which is based on power, money, and pleasure.[A] As this subtle shift occurs, we start to look, sound, and act like the world. We must fight this!

> …keep oneself from being
> polluted by the world.
> James 1:27b

4) As we embrace the world's value system, we begin loving its vices as we become pawns of Satan.

> If anyone loves the world,
> love for the Father is not in them.
> 1 John 2:15b

5) We now fit in, looking no different than non-believers, as we conform to the world and reflect its values. God is distant; our witness is compromised. From an eternal perspective, our life stands for nothing.

> Do not conform to the pattern of this world,
> but be transformed by the renewing of your mind.
> Romans 12:2a

6) As believers, at times we will be disciplined when we sin. It's a form of correction from a loving heavenly Father. Discipline teaches us what is right, as it grows us in wisdom and holiness. It is for our eternal good.[2,3] As we accept the Lord's discipline, He graciously sets us apart from the world.

> We are being disciplined so that we will
> not be…condemned with the world.
> 1 Corinthians 11:32b

Building our lives

Rather than careening down that treacherous, slippery slope, let's closely examine the foundation upon which we build our lives as well as the building materials we are using. This is crucial.

• Our foundation

To live godly lives based on biblical values, we can't live in default mode. We must live with intention, purposely choosing to build our lives upon the foundation of Jesus Christ—the glory of God. This is *the only* solid foundation. It's like building a house upon rock.[4]

Our foundation undergirds everything we stand for. Living in obedience to God is the solid, unshakable foundation we need to weather the storms of life. Faulty foundations—the world's glories—are things such as the quest for more money, the approval of our friends (e.g. how many likes and follows we have on social media), the pursuit of pleasure, indulgence in food, busyness, the latest shopping acquisition, and more comfort or success. The problem: these glories begin to define us.

Most people don't deliberately build their lives upon inferior and faulty foundations. They live with little thought, from one day to the next—one crisis to the next— not realizing their lives are falling apart as they head toward destruction. It comes down to our daily choices that stem from what we allow into our hearts.

We pay a price when we choose the pursuits of the world over the pursuit of God, because the world's values are constantly changing, making an unstable foundation. Anxieties, depression, and fear take hold. Insecurities escalate as our foundation crumbles. We lack joy—and peace—as we live in continual frustration. And exhaustion.

We cannot be careless about the foundation of our lives. Not only does a faulty foundation drive us to misery, but we are also likely to pass this destructive legacy on to our children and grandchildren.

- **Our building materials**

Our building materials must be of lasting and indestructible substances that will hold up under fiery storms—things like God's Word, absolute Truth, prayer, divine wisdom, and God's promises. What we have allowed to mold our character will determine how we withstand our most difficult life challenges.

Even if we have the right foundation, we may choose to use flimsy materials that won't survive—things such as shifting worldly values, human effort, and human wisdom which are worthless! If we build our lives with these materials, our souls will be saved, but barely. All accomplishments done with human effort will be burned up and destroyed; they won't survive the fiery judgment of Christ.

No one can lay any foundation other than
the one already laid, which is Jesus Christ.
If anyone builds on this foundation using
gold, silver, costly stones, wood, hay, or straw,
their work will be shown for what it is,
because the [Judgment] Day will bring it to light.

It will be revealed with fire, and the fire
will test the quality of each person's work.
If it is burned up, the builder will suffer loss
but will be saved—even though only as one
escaping through the flames.

1 Corinthians 3:11-13,15 (brackets mine)

It's very challenging to live our faith *down here* in this fallen world while keeping our focus *up there* in the heavenly realm. Our real home is in Heaven; we only work down here on Earth—for now. This isn't forever!

I thank God for the many ways you impact those around you in your individual mission fields on this earth—reflecting His glory—all the while keeping your eyes set on the eternal!

To God be all glory!

---

[1] Philippians 3:20

[2] Hebrews 12:5b-6a – Do not make light of the Lord's discipline, and do not lose heart when he rebukes you, because the Lord disciplines those he loves.

[3] Hebrews 12:10b-11 – God disciplines us for our good, in order that we may share in his holiness. No discipline seems pleasant at the time, but painful. Later on, however, it produces a harvest of righteousness and peace for those who have been trained by it.

[4] Matthew 7:24-25 – Everyone who hears these words of mine and puts them into practice is like a wise man who built his house on the rock. The rain came down, the streams rose, and the winds blew and beat against that house; yet it did not fall, because it had its foundation on the rock.

20

Our Plumb Line

"If you have integrity, nothing else matters.
If you don't have integrity, nothing else matters."
Alan K. Simpson

Integrity seems to be in short supply these days. People are willing to sell themselves out for some immediate benefit or short-term gain. Many act without thinking of how their actions are shaping their integrity. Life is a series of choices; every choice we make shapes us and refines our integrity.

The Hebrew word for *integrity* in the Old Testament means completeness, perfection, uprightness, and wholeness. In the New Testament, *integrity* also means honesty.[A] It means acting consistently no matter where we are or who we are with.

The greatest person of integrity who ever lived is Jesus Christ. Satan tempted Jesus to compromise His values as He began His ministry. Although He may have been vulnerable, Jesus always came out on top. He is our best example of integrity. Even His disciples noticed. "Teacher, we know that you are a man of integrity. You aren't swayed by others."[1]

When we build a strong integrity, we model Jesus. Because Satan hates Jesus, he attacks people of integrity who follow Him.

The plumb line

Carpenters and builders have used a plumb line for over 4000 years. The plumb bob is the oldest and simplest of tools for establishing plumb—vertical precise balance. It consists of a pointed weight (the plumb bob) that dangles from a string. As a person holds the string at a fixed point, gravity pulls the string taut. When the weight stops swinging and is perfectly still, the line created by the string is plumb—perfectly vertical.

In construction, wood studs, steel beams, concrete pillars, and supporting columns must be precisely plumb to safely support load. This is why skyscrapers don't fall over and bridges don't collapse. If out of plumb by even one degree, the load becomes unbalanced and unstable.

We, too, need a plumb line to function at our best and to remain upright and balanced. We often take on a considerable load of stress. When we live our lives in plumb with Jesus, our load will be one we can shoulder in His strength. Unless we are plumb, we are unstable and unbalanced, at risk of collapsing under the load we must bear on a daily basis. Jesus is our plumb line. What other people do is not our concern; they're not our standard. Wrong is always wrong, no matter who does it.

Called to be like Jesus

As Christians, we are called to be like Jesus. In his book, *Mere Christianity*, C.S. Lewis introduced the idea that Christians should be like little Christs.[B] God calls us to be the plumb line of the Lord as we live with the heart of Christ. It's not all up to us however. The indwelling Holy Spirit is always working to transform us to be more like Jesus as we submit to His will.

We all, who with unveiled faces contemplate
the Lord's glory, are being transformed into his image
with ever-increasing glory,
which comes from the Lord, who is the Spirit.
2 Corinthians 3:18

Living with integrity in our world of evil and immorality at every turn is a challenge. Every righteous act or decision builds and strengthens our integrity. The Holy Spirit helps us accomplish what we cannot on our own. Acting with moral integrity means:

- Keeping our word, no matter what.
- Refusing to compromise on ethical principles.
- Telling the truth, even when a white lie would be easier.
- Coming to work early and working diligently.
- Being honest and trustworthy, not cheating.
- Remaining faithful to our spouse.
- Raising our children with discipline.
- Not taking advantage of people.
- Resisting temptations as they arise.
- Shunning arrogance and seeking humility.
- Not gossiping.
- Not making excuses.
- Being considerate of others.
- Not running from, but meeting problems head on.
- Not building ourselves up by tearing others down.
- Treating our opponents with respect (even if they don't deserve it).
- Not retaliating when attacked.
- Maintaining sexual purity

- Upholding financial responsibility
- Accepting personal accountability.

In essence, integrity means standing for biblical truth, even when it's unpopular. When we devote ourselves to live for the glory of God, our lives will leave an eternal imprint.

Integrity is of critical importance to God; it should be to us as well. In one of his most famous quotes, evangelist Billy Graham says, "When wealth is lost, nothing is lost; when health is lost, something is lost; when character is lost, all is lost."

Author Chinua Achebe asserted, "One of the truest tests of integrity is its blunt refusal to be compromised."[C] It is the commitment to hold the plumb line on biblical truth in society. It is standing for what is right, not compromising moral standards, even when everyone else is caving.[C] Never compromise the integrity of your soul for the sake of the moment. It takes years to build, but only a second to lose.

> I know, my God, that you test the heart
> and are pleased with integrity.
> 1 Chronicles 29:17a

Who or what is your plumb line? Your best friend? The pastor or Bible teacher you greatly admire? A relative? A job title? Your bank account? Anything short of Jesus will disappoint us. Every. Single. Time.

If we use Jesus as our plumb line, our integrity will take care of itself as it reflects Him. And it will bring unprecedented glory to God in the process.

---

[1] Mark 12:14a

21

Get Up!

*I*t all happened so fast!
I never saw it coming!
One moment I was zipping along on the treadmill…and the next…

Wait. I'm getting ahead of myself. Let's start from the beginning.

The morning started out like any other. I had my gym bag packed and was ready to hit the treadmill at the local YMCA. I was feeling determined and focused, ready to crush my workout routine. I stepped on the treadmill and set it to a steep incline. Minutes passed quickly as I power walked with purpose. Feeling the rush of endorphins as I exercised, it was easy to get lost in my reading material.

Suddenly, everything changed!

One way or another, I lost my footing and before I knew it, I found myself tumbling backwards, flailing as I desperately reached for anything to hold onto. All I managed to grab was the stack of papers I was reading. In a split second, I was propelled off the end of my treadmill. Somehow the momentum carried me to the treadmill behind me and I landed on the moving belt with a WHOMP—in a sitting position—papers in hand!

Unfortunately, a lady was using this treadmill at the time, completely unaware of what was to befall her. She reacted quickly as she watched the catastrophe unfold at her feet, her eyes wide with astonishment!

Without delay, she jumped onto the stationary edges of the device—with no time to spare—as I awkwardly passed through her outstretched legs, ducking my head, papers in hand, as I traveled under her. Sheepishly, I looked up to see her eyes brimming with shock as she looked down at me. The machine was heartless as it dumped me off the back end with an audible "plop."

I was a bit dazed and my heart raced as I struggled to regain composure. I felt a surge of embarrassment but broke out in nervous laughter at the absurdity of what had just transpired. A crowd quickly gathered as the gym staff and fellow patrons rushed to my side to make sure I was okay.

Rebecca, our teenage daughter, had come with me that day; she looked absolutely mortified! Of all the embarrassing things a mom can do to humiliate her teenager, I nailed it!

After reassuring the staff I was okay, they slowly dispersed. I cautiously returned to the treadmill to finish my workout routine. Although greatly humbled, I knew I had to keep going and not let this experience get the best of me.

Have you ever had times like this?

One moment you're flying high, adrenaline rushing, on top of the world. The next moment you're stumbling backwards, grasping at anything within reach to break your fall, unsure what went wrong. You planned for success, but things went south quickly.

Did you stumble or fall? Relax. You're just like everyone else. Failure doesn't define you; it simply delays you. It's not your identity!

If you fall, get up. Brush yourself off. Admit and learn from your mistake. You can't change what happened. Let go of the embarrassment. There's nothing you can do about it. Surrender your failure to God and begin again.[1] Success isn't measured by your ability to avoid failure, but by your ability to rise above and move past it. Sometimes failure is the only path to success.

> "You can't go back
> and change the beginning,
> but you can start where you are
> and change the ending."
> C.S. Lewis

Francine Rivers, a best-selling Christian author, has written a series entitled "Sons of Encouragement." Each novella peers into the life of one of five biblical men who stood behind five different heroes of the faith. *The Priest* is about Aaron, the first high priest of Israel. Aaron supported his brother Moses as he led the Israelites out of Egypt and into the Promised Land. Rivers imagines Aaron reached the end of his life feeling greatly discouraged about the many ways he had failed God and let Moses down when it mattered most. He was filled with remorse over his numerous weaknesses and failures. Moses reassured him with wisdom worth integrating into the fabric of our souls,

> The Lord sees our faults, Aaron. He sees our failures and frailty. But what matters to Him is our faith. We have both stumbled, my brother. We have both fallen. And the Lord has lifted us back up with the strength of His mighty hand and remained with us.[A]

Aaron and Moses were amazing men of God and leaders of His people. Yet they both had countless vulnerabilities...ones we all share. Like them, we have also stumbled and fallen, more times than we can count. (At least I have.) But that doesn't make us worthless. What matters most to God is our faith. Faith doesn't take the easy, most convenient, or most comfortable path; faith takes the hard risk for the greatest glory to God. When we surrender to His will and step out in faith through our weaknesses, He will lift us up[2] again…and again…and again. He will transform our current fiasco into something beautiful—something He can use for His glory. His patience is unbelievable! God sees us as we are. And He loves us anyway!

Whether our faith is great or small, God's faithfulness to us is consistent and constant. We can trust what He says in the Bible because we know—without a doubt—that He keeps His word and fulfills His promises. Our eternal destiny is secure. We can rest in God's unchanging nature.

"Be of good cheer.
Do not think of today's failures…
you will succeed if you persevere;
and you will find joy in overcoming obstacles."
Helen Keller

It's a new day! Get up; brush yourself off. Begin again. Today is a fresh opportunity to move forward, trust God, and reflect His goodness and glory!

One step at a time!

---

[1] James 1:12a, NASB – Blessed is a man who perseveres under trial.
[2] Isaiah 41:10 – So do not fear, for I am with you; do not be dismayed, for I am your God. I will strengthen you and help you; I will uphold you with my righteous right hand."

22

Our Hidden Strength

Sometimes I get discouraged as I consider the many ways I fall short. I wonder how I will accomplish what I need to do—and do it well. After all, what I have on my plate right now isn't what I'm gifted to do. I am ill-equipped.

Can you relate?

Remember the great apostle, Paul? He had weaknesses too. We don't think of Paul as having shortcomings because he did everything so well and appeared self-confident. But Paul had a number of weaknesses and he happily boasted about them! That runs counter to everything in us. I'm more likely to hide my weaknesses from others or suppress them deep inside. Not gloat over them to others.

Paul didn't get upset about his faults. Nor did he lament over or get discouraged by them. Instead, he put them on display, essentially telling God, "God, I can't do this. I need you. I trust you to show up. Here are my weaknesses. Do your thing." Then he watched God show up in power in ways that boggled his mind!

Our weaknesses, infused with God's strength, reflect Jesus to the world. That's what makes our weaknesses so powerful! Christ's "upside-down" principle of being stronger in our *weaknesses* than in our natural *strengths* makes no sense. But in God's Kingdom, it makes perfect sense.

What does this have to do with me?

Everything!

If I had only strengths (and no weaknesses), I'd be like a HUGE army with impressive military prowess and advanced weaponry, facing only fledgling enemies; I'd always knock out easy wins because I was so powerful. Not very impressive, is it? Nor very exciting. These victories, in fact, would be terribly predictable—ho hum—quite boring.

Instead, I'm like an army of few men with no military expertise, and no weapons—facing a foreboding rival. Much like a Bible hero, Gideon. He had a large army which dwindled down until he was outnumbered 450:1. And their weapons? Well…they each had a trumpet, an empty jar, and a lighted torch. No swords. No bullets. No bombs. No bows and arrows. Not even a pocket knife!

How about you?

What are *you* facing this week? What challenge looms mightily in front of *you* right now? Is it draining *your* strength and resources? Is it playing on *your* insecurities? Are *you* too exhausted and depleted to pull together a battle plan? Are *you* feeling ill-equipped? Perhaps *you're* feeling threatened? Are *you* nervous? Do *you* feel too weak to fight?

Step back a minute! Where's your focus? This isn't about *you*. It's about God! Let's change the focus. Your situation belongs to God. Give it to Him and watch Him turn insecurities into confidence, weaknesses into strengths, and fears into victories.

As we step out in faith, He strengthens us with the skills and the wisdom we'll need to face challenges up ahead. God sustains, comforts, leads, and equips us. He has not overlooked us.

The joy of the Lord

> The joy of the Lord is your strength.
> Nehemiah 8:10

We draw strength from many sources including people, our jobs, and our abilities. But when push comes to shove, our so-called strength is simply weakness; it amounts to nothing! Strength from the Lord, however, is entirely different! One way He gives us strength is through His joy.

The world gives us happiness—short-lived pleasure based on our external circumstances. Joy, however, is a spiritual fruit—a deep-seated lasting pleasure which gives us the strength to persevere through whatever we are facing. Nothing in this world will bring us joy—only Jesus and a relationship with Him. Joy is NOT of this world! It is supernatural. It contains power. It's not just a feeling. The sinner has no reason for joy. But the *forgiven* sinner has every reason to rejoice because the power of the Lord restores him and transforms his sorrow into joy.

When we believe what God says in His Word and live our lives upon this foundation, a holy boldness—an unconventional confidence—and a deep-seated joy will result. They will transcend the blinding storms we encounter. Augustine said it best. "God does not choose a person because he is worthy but by the act of choosing him, He makes him worthy."

Remember God? He's still there—waiting to be invited to your battle—your challenge. But he doesn't want to be "one of the guys." He wants to be the Commander-in-Chief…because He has already formulated the strategy for success! Face it: you don't have what it takes to fight your battles and win.

So, here's the question…

Will you go it alone or will you align with God? He's got your back; you can trust Him. Whatever pitiful talents, resources, and weaknesses you have—they will be enough because God fights for you![1]

Wherever you are, God has you there for a purpose. This is a test of your faith. God knows your weaknesses, yet those don't concern Him. Will you admit your weaknesses and humbly give them to God? He won't fix something you hold onto and complain about. When you open your fist and surrender them to Him in prayer, He releases His supernatural power to strengthen you *through* them so you can succeed. And you get to see His strength when He carries you through what you can't handle alone.

> "Instead of letting inadequacy hinder you from obeying,
> let it drive you to your knees so you can arise
> with renewed insight and power."
> Dr. Charles Stanley

Left to our own devices, we are on a trajectory of being what we've always been. We surely don't want that! Nor does God—He wants more for us! He has a better plan for our lives. Submit to His will and walk with Him. Don't forget to praise His Holy name, giving all glory to Him for the victory to come. God will hold you in the palm of His hand and guide you every step of the way… And you'll see His grace is truly sufficient![2]

---

[1] Exodus 14:14 – The Lord will fight for you; you need only to be still.

[2] 2 Corinthians 12:9a – He said to me, 'My grace is sufficient for you, for my power is made perfect in weakness.'

23

Our Legacy

Where are you? How did you get there?

Every action we take leads us down a path to somewhere and each action began in our minds with a thought. What we put into our minds determines what comes out in our thoughts, then in our words and actions.

Ralph Waldo Emerson stated,

> "Sow a thought, reap an action.
> Sow an action, reap a habit.
> Sow a habit, reap a character.
> Sow a character, reap a destiny."

I'd like to take this one step further:

> Sow a destiny, reap a legacy.

Our destiny shapes our legacy. Our legacy—what we leave behind when we die—is the impact we have had on people and places during our lifetime. Essentially, it's the mark we leave on the world. Face it—we all want to be remembered when we die. When we stop to consider the kind of legacy we want to leave behind, our lives take on fresh meaning and purpose.

Our thoughts

Our legacy is rooted in our thoughts. If we want to change our legacy, we begin by changing our thoughts. This requires intention. Paul provides insight as to how to do this.

> Whatever is true, whatever is honorable,
> whatever is just, whatever is pure,
> whatever is lovely,
> whatever is commendable,
> if there is any excellence,
> if there is anything worthy of praise,
> think about these things.
> Philippians 4:8, ESV

When we consider all the amazing things we can think about and the long-term consequences that can result from our thoughts, it's daunting. To succeed in this effort, we must intentionally focus on Jesus and allow the Holy Spirit, not the world, to control the direction our minds take and the subsequent thoughts that result.

> The mind controlled by the Spirit
> is life and peace.
> Romans 8:6b

Our thoughts contain tremendous power! Left under our imperfect and flawed human control, they can quickly take over and destroy peace with our anxieties and fears. Through prayer, we have access to the power of the Holy Spirit to help us regain control and steer our lives in a positive direction.

Take captive every thought
to make it obedient to Christ.
2 Corinthians 10:5b

As we surrender to God in prayer, He will help us focus our minds and thoughts on what is good, pure, and edifying as we eliminate impure, harmful, and toxic input. This is a choice for freedom as our thoughts reflect our values and in turn, shape our lives. The result: peace and joy.

As a thought enters our mind, we must ask ourselves if it is true, honorable, just, pure, lovely, commendable, excellence, or praiseworthy. If not, discard it, and walk away. It's not from God.

Some examples are:

- It's hopeless.
- I'm worthless.
- I dread being with him.
- He will never amount to anything.
- I know I'm going to fail.
- I'm stupid.
- She is a hot mess.
- My husband deserves better.
- I can't do anything right.
- Things will never change.
- I'll always be this miserable.

Thoughts such as these are from the enemy of our soul—never God! God doesn't condemn,[1] but has our absolute best at heart.

What occupies your thoughts?

Perhaps it's time to examine your thoughts and bring them under the control of Christ. Every thought leads to a decision that takes you down one of two paths:

- A path of destructive pessimism, criticism, and harmful outcomes, or
- A path filled with constructive optimism, goodness, and peaceful outcomes.

Adjusting the way you think will change the direction of your life!

> "When you're born, you look like your parents.
> But when you die, you look like your decisions."
> Dr. Crawford Loritts

If you continue on your current path with the habits and character traits you've developed, what legacy will you leave behind for your loved ones?

- Do you reflect the Lord or the world as you live each day?
- Will your legacy be one that glorifies God?
- Will it be a legacy that points to Jesus and leads to eternal salvation?

It may be time to rethink things.

---

[1] Romans 8:1 – There is now no condemnation for those who are in Christ Jesus.

24

～◯～

Shattering the Darkness

We are familiar with the creation story. "In the beginning," we learn, "God created the heavens and the earth."[1] The earth was formless and empty; thick, impenetrable darkness hung heavy as it spread out, laying claim to every bit of the immeasurable expanse, covering the waters. And God spent six days creating...

The Holy Spirit hovered gingerly over the waters, patiently waiting in eager expectation for God to speak. And that He did!

Do you remember the first thing God declared after creating the heavens and the Earth? His thundering voice reverberated with authority and power throughout the vast space. "Let there be light."[2]

And it was so.

On the surface, this may not seem terribly noteworthy. Oh, but it is! It's fascinating to consider that God didn't create the stars, the Sun, or the Moon until the fourth day. How could a brilliance of light burst forth with such magnificence in the absence of celestial bodies? Most Bible scholars believe this unique light was God and the light of His glory. His glory ruled over the inky darkness, dispelling it in an instant!

When God created Adam and Eve, He placed them in a paradise to live—the Garden of Eden—until Satan, in the form of a great serpent, showed up. Satan deceived them into committing the first sin, and the world spiraled into darkness as Adam and Eve were cast out of the garden. We have been living in spiritual darkness ever since, which clouds every aspect of our existence. The great prophet, Isaiah, paints a powerful picture of overwhelming gloom.

Darkness covers the earth
and thick darkness is over the peoples.
Isaiah 60:2a

The darkness (referring to the sin that consumes the human race) is so thick and heavy we can't see beyond it; it covers everything. Satan, the ruler of the darkness, planned it this way to blind the world from discerning reality. It has been a constant battle between good and evil, generation after generation, ever since then. Thankfully, God doesn't leave us to wallow and flounder in this murky darkness.

But the LORD rises upon you
and his glory appears over you.
Isaiah 60:2b

From a state of total despair, a sudden explosion of glory pierced the heavens as Jesus Christ, the Son of God was born! Jesus, the light of the world, split open the darkness with profound power and blinding brilliance!

God is light;
in him there is no darkness at all.
1 John 1:5b

The entire climate of the heavens and Earth changed in an instant! There is no darkness so thick that God's glory cannot penetrate it! Tragically we didn't recognize His glory and we nailed it to a cross. May the Lord forgive us!

In the dark, good and evil often look alike, but in the light, they can be clearly distinguished. Many people live in the darkness of their sin, making excuses for their immoral choices. They fear the light because it exposes their sin.

> "We can easily forgive a child
> who is afraid of the dark,
> the real tragedy of life is
> when men are afraid of the light."
> Plato

When God's Word is not our standard of holiness and rightness, all moral choices appear fuzzy, with the line between good and evil blurred. Isaiah cautioned, "Woe to those who call evil good and good evil, who put darkness for light and light for darkness."[3] God warns us against the peril of confusing the two.

Today, the world is full of darkness because sin runs rampant; the darkness is so thick it completely covers the earth and all people.

> "God's light will overcome the total darkness
> that has covered the world since the fall
> and kept countless millions in spiritual darkness."
> Tony Evans

Darkness cannot exist in the presence of light. As such, carnal sin cannot exist in the presence of divine light—our holy God.

> The light shines in the darkness,
> and the darkness has not overcome it.
> John 1:5

Jesus Christ is the Creator of life and His life brings light to mankind. As we walk with Jesus, He lights our path ahead, one step at a time, so we can avoid stumbling in the darkness of sin. Only the light of Christ can expose and dispel the darkness of sin and evil in our lives.

There will certainly be dark times when it seems like evil is winning. Don't be fooled! It is only an illusion; evil never has the last word!

In our humanity, we are powerless against evil. The cross is the only tool capable of defeating evil. The cross—a symbol of death that may *seem* evil—is actually the means of our salvation *from* the evil. The cross conquers evil (and thus sin and death) so glory can regain its dominion over the world that it had at creation.

And then there was morning

After every day God created, we see this phrase, "And there was evening, and there was morning—the first day" etc. Notice the day didn't end with night; it ended with morning. Every night is followed by a morning. Each morning's light infiltrates the dark night of our soul. God brings light into our darkness because light drives out the darkness. The light wins! Every. Single. Time.

Let's determine to walk in the light of our faith. When we do, there will be no confusing choices, no hopeless situations, and no desperate chaos because the light of Christ brings revelation, order, peace, and hope.

Praise be to God!

The ending—which is really the beginning...

The Bible opens in Genesis 1 with the light of God bursting forth, penetrating the darkness of Heaven and Earth. And the Bible ends in the final chapter of Revelation with the light of God illuminating the new heaven and the new earth in dazzling brilliance with the eternal radiance of His splendor and glory! One glorious day, God's presence will be the only light we will need.

> There will be no more night.
> They will not need the light of a lamp
> or the light of the sun,
> for the Lord God will give them light.
> And they will reign for ever and ever.
> Revelation 22:5

There will be no more sin—evil—sorrow—fear—pain—tears. All GONE! All confusion will be instantly replaced with total clarity and understanding.

Are you reflecting His light?

It's all about God's glory.

Don't miss it!

---

[1] Genesis 1:1

[2] Genesis 1:3a

[3] Isaiah 5:20a

25

Where Is Your Battleground?

*A*re you weary from constantly battling something? Are you discouraged—disheartened? Do you feel drained? Is your hope fading fast? It's time to consider the way you battle.

The first battle on Earth was between Eve and a serpent—a snake—that had entered the Garden of Eden. Snakes are cunning animals. If you've ever watched a snake, you know they are unpredictable and cold-hearted. They seek their prey with an intensity that is chilling.

Enter the eagle

This majestic bird will sometimes go after the snake, but the eagle is smart and calculating. It employs a tactic worth emulating. The eagle wisely chooses not to fight the snake on the ground. Instead, it picks it up and flies off with it into the sky. By doing so, the eagle is changing the battleground. You see, the snake has no ability, no power, and absolutely no control in the air. It is helpless, weak, and vulnerable—unlike on the ground where it is strong, adept, and very deadly. When the time is right, the eagle releases the snake into the sky where it plummets to its death.^ In the sky, the eagle wins.

We can learn a lot from the eagle.

Has the enemy slithered its way into your world? Is he wreaking havoc in your life? The enemy is Satan, the "prince of the air."[1] (Satan is referred to as prince because Christ is the King.)

Likely, the word "air" refers to the unseen realm where Satan and his demons dwell, move about, and scheme to bring about our downfall. It probably also includes the air of our world.

Has he invaded your home—your workplace—your thoughts? Satan has his way here on Earth, albeit for a limited period of time. This is his turf; the Earth is this serpent's battleground. We are out of our element in this world.

Change your battleground

We should never battle Satan in his element. And certainly not in our own power. We will lose every time.

When the heaviness of the world threatens to overtake us, let's not back down in defeat. But rise up! To fight effectively, we must take the battle onto different terrain where Satan isn't effective. How? Through prayer! By praying, we enter the heavenly realm where God reigns supreme, and we immerse ourselves in His living presence. Our prayers open the floodgates of Heaven and release spiritual power as God battles for us there.

Our battles are best fought in that realm with spiritual weapons, not down here with worldly weapons; whatever human abilities or earthly authority we may have are ineffective in spiritual battles.

This is why prayer is so powerful—our most valuable resource! Only spiritual weapons will tear down the opposition. Human methods used to battle demonic forces are doomed to fail.

You will not have to fight this battle.
Take up your positions; stand firm and see
the deliverance the Lord will give you.
2 Chronicles 20:17a

Change battlegrounds and invite God to take charge through your heartfelt and focused prayers. In the heavenlies, God wins. And so do you!

Be bold and specific in your requests to God. Tell Him what's going on: your struggles, your fears, your worries, your anxieties. Unless you are involving your heavenly Father, you aren't using all the strength and power available to you.

Stop allowing the enemy to keep you on his level and control the battle. It's time to take back control.

Don't be caught cornered by the mighty serpent who seeks to steal your joy, kill your self-esteem, and destroy your purpose![2] He will always try to keep you on his level as he throws your world into a tailspin of unbridled chaos and anxiety, rendering you completely ineffective. Satan is never passive; he is always scheming.

Instead, make everything that stands against you stand before our living God. An army of angels is ready to be dispatched; just sound the alarm and summon your Father! Battle wisely. Take it to the spiritual realm where your victory is secure.

Be aware; keep your eyes peeled—do not let the enemy set one foot into your world. When he tries, you know what to do...

---

[1] Ephesians 2:2, ESV.
[2] John 10:10a – The thief comes only to steal and kill and destroy.

26

The Peace of Jesus

A major art gallery held a competition. Artists were asked to paint a picture exemplifying peace. The artists gathered their paints, brushes, and canvases and began to create their masterpieces.

The competition was grueling, but at last, the judges narrowed it down to just two finalists. One artist painted a gorgeous sunset with the Sun descending over a serene lake. It was idyllic—tranquil. Gazing at the painting had a very calming effect. This work of art was awarded second place.

The winning masterpiece initially had the judges baffled. This painting depicted a powerful, raging storm. The sky was ominous—a mosaic of shifting grays in foreboding hues as billowing, steely clouds commanded the horizon. Flashes of lightning zigzagged across the heavens as the force of the storm churned below. Waves crashed against the rocky cliff walls along the shore. One could almost hear wind howling and cracks of thunder while gazing at the painting. Things looked chaotic. Until…

In the center of the painting, a tiny dove sat on a nest within a cleft of the rocky boulders, her babies tucked safely underneath her, asleep. As the storm erupted around her, she was protected and safe. Despite the raging storm, the mother bird was at peace and her babies were sleeping.

"Peace in the Midst of the Storm" by Jack E. Dawson

His departure was imminent

Jesus spent His last three years on Earth doing life with His disciples. He saw and experienced their world—all the hostility, strife, adversity, tragedy, and difficult people. He observed the fear in their eyes during a severe storm. He felt their anxiety and dread when the religious elite oppressed them. He saw how the blind and lame were mistreated and disrespected. He witnessed the corrupt political system and brutality of the Roman officials. He beheld the hatred and evil that permeated their world. Peace was nearly impossible with the violence and callousness of the culture.

His own life was far from easy. Jesus was subjected to much hatred, evil, and contempt. He knew His disciples, then and now, would be too.[1,2,3] He knew we would suffer rejection, ridicule, and persecution because of our alliance with Him. And we'd be tempted to pursue false worldly peace—things like money, status, materialism, popularity, or power. Or be inclined to believe peace can be found by escaping stress through food, alcohol, or drugs. Or by burying our heads in TV, internet, or video games. These temporal pursuits offer only a false sense of security and short-lived freedom. They solve nothing.

Jesus knew we would need encouragement to persevere through life's relentless challenges. We would crave a deep, abiding peace to sustain us—a holy respite from the evil darkness of the world.

The Prince of Peace offers a gift

Peace is a major theme in God's Word—mentioned 420 times in the KJV. As the Prince of Peace,[4] His reign is unlike any other ruler who ever served because it is not characterized by pride, power, or dominance, but by a quiet, confident peace.

Jesus was painfully aware that His departure from this world was fast approaching. With loving compassion, He looked tenderly upon His disciples and thought of those who were living and those yet to be born. He thought of you. He thought of me. He wanted to protect and satisfy our deep-seated craving for peace.

Shortly before His death, with His disciples gathered around Him, He promised to send the Holy Spirit to live in believers; they would never be alone![5] The Spirit would grow in them, producing nine spiritual fruits as they walked in faith; one of these fruits was divine peace.[6] He offers us the same extraordinary peace!

> "Peace I leave with you; my peace I give you.
> I do not give to you as the world gives.
> Do not let your hearts be troubled
> and do not be afraid."
> John 14:27

His peace comes with a command. Essentially, "Don't get stressed out and allow fear to take hold." Whether we face persecution, illness, failure, or loss, Jesus can deliver us from the fear associated with it. Even in our darkest moments, we can experience an inner calm—His incomprehensible peace.

Peace is a product of surrender, not control

Life will always be filled with conflict, suffering, evil, loss, and pain because for a short time,[7] God allows Satan free reign of this world. But as Christians, we don't have to swim in the turbulent waters of anxiety and despair. When we refuse to allow the busyness and stress of life to shift our focus off Christ, we can experience His abiding peace in every situation. We can thrive when life is turned upside down because this peace is rooted in our Prince of Peace. "He [Jesus] is our peace."[8]

This is where free will comes in. If we choose to be filled with the Holy Spirit each day, peace will follow. "The mind governed by the Spirit is life and peace."[9] A peace-filled heart is the result of surrendering to and trusting God, knowing that He has overcome the world—not with power, but with sacrifice—and therefore He has overcome our challenges as well.

If we neglect this, Satan will fill us with anxiety, fear, and insecurity. Billy Graham revealed that he asked the Holy Spirit to take his life every day and use it for His glory. What a great idea!

Living peace amidst the storm

Ed Dobson, author and pastor of a megachurch in Grand Rapids, Michigan struggled with fear and anxiety after he was diagnosed with ALS (Lou Gehrig's disease).

He admitted he became so obsessed with his disease, his future, and getting healed that he lost his focus. A friend who was a pastor advised, "Get lost in the wonder of God, and who knows what He will do for you."[A] Dobson came to a realization:

> I needed to shift my focus from myself to my creator. And I shouldn't focus on God's power to heal me…I should focus on the all-around wonder of God and spend more time with Him each day without the goal of receiving healing…I needed to trust Him with my life not because I was sick, but because I should trust Him that way always.[B]

He went on to say,

> Every day is a gift. Every day I am trusting in God and in His grace. Every day I try to live life to its fullest. I try not to worry about tomorrow. I try to focus on today. And I know that God and His grace are sufficient for the moment I find myself in. When I wake up tomorrow, whatever the challenges, I know God will be there and will provide His grace….This is my strength.[C]

Peace in the storm. Dobson lived this kind of peace. And he reflected it to thousands upon thousands who were looking for hope and direction in the midst of their own personal storms.

Guarding our hearts and minds

Do not be anxious about anything,
but in every situation, by prayer and petition,
with thanksgiving, present your requests to God.

143

And the peace of God,
which transcends all understanding,
will guard your hearts and your minds in Christ Jesus.
Philippians 4:5-7

The word Paul used for *guard* is a military term, meaning a battalion that safeguards against enemy attacks. God's peace is like a garrison, guarding and protecting our hearts and minds when the enemies of worry and fear try to invade. He replaces our inner turmoil with a quiet trust and calm that are unshakable.

You will keep in perfect peace
those whose minds are steadfast,
because they trust in you.
Isaiah 26:3

Perfect peace comes from having a steadfast mind—steady, unshaken, focused, unchanging—which trusts in the Lord. No matter what. Claim your peace amid your trial. God won't deliver us from every trial; if He did, we would never grow to be like Jesus. He didn't deliver Jesus from every trial either. If God doesn't remove your trial, it's for an eternal benefit.

Our light and momentary troubles
are achieving for us an eternal glory
that far outweighs them all.
2 Corinthians 4:17

Because God's love for us is so powerful, we can trust Him in our suffering. We do not slog through alone; our footing is held secure because our suffering is under the control of an all-powerful and all-loving God. It has meaning and purpose in His eternal plan. And the infinite glory we will experience will be immeasurably greater than our current suffering.[10] The wait for Heaven will be worth it.

When peace is impossible

Peace is impossible when we choose to live with active sin, rejecting God. We will no longer have His hand of protection covering us. Fear and anxiety will rule as He allows us to go our own way, without Him, into the perils of the world. It's a dangerous place to be. God takes sin very seriously!

Are you in the midst of a raging storm?

Peace is not the absence of the storm; it is the calm in the midst of the storm. No matter what you're dealing with, God is on the throne, sheltering you with His peace as you trust Him. Step away from your chaos toward the Peacemaker Himself.

> Whoever dwells in the shelter of the Most High
> will rest in the shadow of the Almighty...
> He will cover you with his feathers,
> and under his wings you will find refuge.
> Psalm 91:1,4

The bird from the painting tucked herself in the cleft of the rock as she rested in the storm, secure. We, too, can tuck ourselves in the cleft of the Rock (Jesus is our Rock[11]) and rest, secure in the protective embrace of our loving God. When you surrender to Him, peace will reign as the

145

storms of life rage over and around you. He will guard your heart and mind from anxiety.

When the world looks at you, they will know that you have what their souls yearn for: a life ruled by peace.

What a legacy!

May you experience His deep, abiding peace within you as you trust God through your tears and your fears. Let His presence envelop you in His comfort, giving you the freedom to live with abandon and confidence. You are not at the mercy of your anxieties.

The best benefit of all—as we live out His peace in the midst of our chaos, it's proof that "the one who is in you is greater than the one who is in the world."[12] His glory is on full display—reflecting off us with blinding intensity to those desperate for hope.

---

[1] John 16:33a – I have told you these things, so that in me you may have peace.

[2] 1 John 3:13, TLB – Don't be surprised…if the world hates you.

[3] John 15:18-19 – If the world hates you, keep in mind that it hated me first. If you belonged to the world, it would love you as its own. As it is, you do not belong to the world, but I have chosen you out of the world. That is why the world hates you.

[4] Isaiah 9:6

[5] Ephesians 1:13b – When you believed, you were marked in him with a seal, the promised Holy Spirit.

[6] Galatians 5:22-23 – The fruit of the Spirit is love, joy, peace…

[7] John 16:33b – In this world you will have trouble. But take heart! I have overcome the world.

[8] Ephesians 2:14 (brackets mine)

[9] Romans 8:6b

[10] Romans 8:18 – Our present sufferings are not worth comparing with the glory that will be revealed in us.

[11] Deuteronomy 32:4 – He is the Rock, his works are perfect, and all his ways are just.

[12] 1 John 4:4b

27

Living Water

Have you ever been thirsty? Really thirsty? So parched that it overrides every other thought or feeling? This was not an uncommon experience in Israel, especially in the south where the Negev Desert encompasses the terrain. Although a place of amazing beauty, the desert's intense heat and parched earth make life a challenge. Water in this area is a priceless commodity and the pursuit of it a daily challenge.

About 600 years before Christ, Israel was facing tough times. The northern kingdom had been taken into Assyrian captivity and the southern kingdom was immersed in idolatry. The country was in shambles, so God sent a young man, about 20 years old, to be a prophet to His people; his name was Jeremiah. His first assignment was to deliver this message from the Lord to the people.

> My people have committed two sins:
> They have forsaken me,
> the spring of living water,
> and have dug their own cisterns,
> broken cisterns that cannot hold water.
> Jeremiah 2:13

If you're like me and weren't raised on a farm, you may not know that a cistern is basically an underground storage tank that collects and holds run-off water. Cisterns in biblical times were pits dug into limestone rock that collected rainwater.[A]

The best source of water was fresh and running, such as that which flows from a spring or stream. Water from a cistern was considered the worst source as it was stagnant and collected leaves, mosquito larvae, mud, bird droppings, urine, and a whole host of other unhealthy things.[B]

The people of that day understood the striking imagery in the Lord's words spoken by Jeremiah. Although God had delivered Israel from Egypt to the land of milk and honey, the Israelites had forgotten Him and sought after false gods. They essentially traded the spring of fresh, flowing water (Living Water) for the worst water source (muddy cisterns) only capable of collecting stale, stagnant, contaminated water. And the cisterns often cracked, and water leaked out. The cisterns were pretty much worthless! Yet the people chose these homemade cisterns.

The meaning was clear. They chose to rely on and, in essence, worship other gods and even themselves rather than the Living God!

Surely, we are more advanced and sophisticated today, aren't we? Hardly! When we are careless in nurturing our faith, neglectful in pursuing our relationship with Christ, lax in studying His Word, and disobedient in our choices, we are turning away from God.

God promises to lead us to living water, yet we often tell Him, "Thanks anyway, but I've got it covered. I have my own thing going over here. In fact, I found a shovel. I think I'll just dig my own cistern." And we start digging our own worldly cisterns, the contents of which promise to fill and refresh us, but never deliver. We turn our backs on God to satisfy our thirst with poor substitutes such as the idols of materialism, entertainment, alcohol, immorality, false religions, and self-dependence! How prideful.

All idols are like consuming salt water. They never truly satisfy thirst; we keep coming back for more because our thirst is never quenched. Only God's Living Water satisfies deep abiding thirst. Looking at the ocean, it would seem drinking it would quench our thirst. It takes little time, however, to realize it's futile; we come away more thirsty than before.

New life

Life is often like living in a desert—many parched souls seeking relief from the intense heated pressures of their world. Lives hang in the balance as people make decisions which will impact the rest of their lives. Many thirst for pure, uncontaminated, refreshing water. Maybe no one has shown them how to find the endless supply of living water. Perhaps no one has explained that living water from God is pure, satisfying, and life-giving. And even better—it flows from a constant stream that will never dry up!

Whatever the case, too many people are relentlessly digging, crafting their own cisterns to collect the lifeless, stale, dangerous waters of the world. They have heard such things as alcohol, drugs, popularity, sex, materialism, power, envy, and the approval of others will quench that unbearable thirst within their souls. They are consumed with and addicted to social media. The world is confusing and corrupt. They don't know who they can trust or where to turn. And to make matters worse, they find their cisterns cracked. So, they remain thirsty! And they continue on... empty.

Who can we send into the world to tell them that digging their own cistern is a bad plan—and cisterns break?

That it doesn't matter how hard they work or how fast they dig, it will never solve their problems. God will never help us dig our own cistern no matter how frustrated we get.

We must be willing to seek out and lead people to the Source of the true Living Water…the only place where they can find true joy, fulfillment, and refreshment. For Christ is our Living Water—the source of all blessings. We must thirst for His sweet presence.

One day perhaps we will find hordes of people nourished by the river of life which flows freely, producing such rich fruit that high school, college, and workplaces will no longer be life-threatening deserts, but a fountain teeming with Life eternal!

To God be all glory and honor!!!

For further reflection

Whoever drinks the water
I give them will never thirst.
Indeed, the water I give them
will become in them a spring of water
welling up to eternal life.
John 4:14

Jesus stood and said in a loud voice,
"Let anyone who is thirsty come to me and drink.
Whoever believes in me,
as Scripture has said,
rivers of living water will flow
from within them."
John 7:37-38

Living Water

For the Lamb at the center of the throne
will be their shepherd;
he will lead them to springs of living water.
Revelation 7:17a

———

Then the angel showed me the river of
the water of life, as clear as crystal,
flowing from the throne of God and of the Lamb.
Revelation 22:1

———

The Spirit and the bride say, "Come!"
And let the one who hears say, "Come!"
Let the one who is thirsty come;
and let the one who wishes
take the free gift of the water of life.
Revelation 22:17

28

A Risk Worth Taking

Travel with me back in time...back 2000 years in Israel. There you will find Peter in a boat on the Sea of Galilee with the other disciples, battling a raging storm in the pitch black of night. Although a seasoned fisherman, Peter is facing a tempest, the intensity of which he's never seen. And he is petrified!

But take a closer look. You see, Peter was unusual. He had the courage to look beyond the margins of his life story—beyond his fears—to find hope in the midst of the storm in the form of Jesus walking on the water, telling him, "Come."[1] Peter chose to step out of the boat into the tumultuous waves to pursue that hope, regardless of the risk.

He chose to be with Jesus in the squall rather than stay within the confines of the boat. It was a risk—the biggest risk of his life! But it was one he was willing to take.

Too many people are the other eleven disciples who look longingly beyond the edge of the boat—the edge of their story—but are so focused on the waves of the culture that their view of Jesus is obscured. Meanwhile, the storms of life rage on. The howling winds of temptation are fierce. The crashing waves of the culture are so deafening they can't hear Jesus calling to them. The water is unrelenting—pounding, threatening to tear apart their security. The water is pouring over the sides of the boat. But even more frightening is the thought of leaving the boat. Who is this Guy who calls, "Come." Can He be trusted?

What does your life story look like?

What fears are pounding you, threatening to tear apart everything you hold secure? Is the water level rising; do you feel you will drown?

Someone stands in the midst of your tempest—a hand extended—Someone who cares. Will you leave the false comfort of what you know and brave the raging waters beyond the familiar—with Jesus? He awaits your decision. He hopes you leave behind the storm of your emotions and cross the boundaries of your story to join Him. He can quell your storm with His extravagant grace.

God knows your story—every jot and tittle. He has the power to deliver you safely to salvation—to a life of abundance and unparalleled, lasting joy. Don't let your eyes stray to the turbulent waves. Pray for the courage to stay focused on Jesus. A wise man once observed, "You can choose courage, or you can choose comfort; you cannot choose both."

It's worth the risk

Ask Peter. He stepped out in faith and took a risk. And it paid off. He was later given great authority and became the first leader of the early Church. Peter performed many miracles in the name of Jesus.

It's time to leave your boat of perceived comfort and take a risk of faith. It's better to be with Jesus in the squall and waves than without Him in the boat. When you choose to take a risk with God, it will change the trajectory of your life. You will never be the same.

Will you seek other terrified, battered souls as well and encourage them to step out of their boat and go to Jesus, leaving behind their worldly comforts? Help them brave the torrential spiritual storm threatening to sweep them away.

Evangelist Billy Graham once noted, "Courage is contagious. When a brave man takes a stand, the spines of others are often stiffened."[A] Step out of the boat—then bring others with you to Jesus who stands waiting—calling, "Come."

(Please read the full story in Matthew 14:22-33.)

---

[1] Matthew 14:29

29

Mysteries of the Gates

The year was 586 B.C. God had been patient with the Israelites for a long time, but they continued to sin and worship idols, despite many warnings. God had endured enough. He couldn't allow the people He loved to go on like this any longer. To get their attention, He disciplined them by using Babylon (modern-day Iraq) to destroy Jerusalem. The city and the temple were set on fire. The walls of this magnificent city were torn down—widespread destruction.

The Babylonian soldiers looted everything of value and killed hundreds of thousands of Jews, including priests and children. Some escaped but were soon captured. They were bound together, chained, and led to Babylon, likely a four-month trek, taking a route around the Arabian desert—about 900 miles.[A]

And there they lived in what has been called the Babylonian Captivity. Seventy years later, the Jews were released from exile. They returned to their precious homeland to find it in ruins! The people banded together and rebuilt the temple in 516 B.C., but it held little of the opulence and magnificence of the first temple.

Yet, a great problem remained. There was no wall around the city of Jerusalem. The people lived unprotected for the next seventy years. They and their God had become a laughingstock to surrounding countries. They were vulnerable to enemy attack, humiliated, and devastated. The crumbling destroyed wall was a symbol of the brokenness of the people.

Enter Nehemiah 142 years later. Nehemiah wasn't a priest, a prophet, or a ruler; he was simply an ordinary man. But his heart was burdened with the same things that burdened God's heart. In 445 B.C., he led the charge to rebuild the wall, despite overwhelming odds. What an enormous task!

The wall and gates

The wall surrounding Jerusalem consisted of ten sections separated by ten gates. Each gate represents a different aspect of our Christian walk with God. The order and location of each gate are very specific and provide insight into our journey with God.

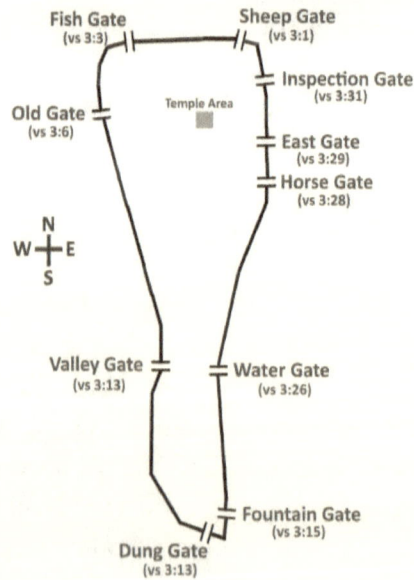

Jerusalem's Walls & Gates
In the days of Nehemiah (Nehemiah Chapter 3)

aa

Construction begins!

Let's take a walk around the city counterclockwise.

The Sheep Gate

*Eliashib the high priest and his fellow priests went to work
and rebuilt the Sheep Gate.
They dedicated it and set its doors in place.*[1]

―――――

The Sheep Gate, situated near the Temple, is the first gate. Eliashib, the high priest, and other priests rebuilt this gate as it held special significance to them. Sheep and lambs to be used in the sacrifice for sin offerings were brought into the Temple through this gate. It was near the market where sheep were sold and sacrifices were washed.[B]

This gate represents the starting point in our Christian life—the realization that Jesus is the Lamb of God who takes away the sins of the world; He is also the High Priest of the New Covenant. Undergirding everything is this principle: out of death comes life.

The Fish Gate

*The Fish Gate was rebuilt by the sons of Hassenaah.
They laid its beams and put its doors and bolts and bars in place.*[2]

―――――

The merchants brought fish from Tyre or the Sea of Galilee through this gate to sell at the fish market.[B] Fishing is often used as a symbol of witnessing to others. Jesus said to His disciples,

"Follow me, and I will make you
fishers of men."
Matthew 4:19, KJV

159

Once we grasp Jesus's sacrifice, we want to tell others. The Fish Gate, now called The Damascus Gate, reminds us to point people to the Lamb of God—represented by The Sheep Gate. Coming to Jesus is where salvation occurs.

The Old Gate

The Jeshanah Gate was repaired by Joiada
son of Paseah and Meshullam son of Besodeiah.
They laid its beams and put its doors and bolts and bars in place. [3]

This gate was the main entrance into the old city of Jerusalem[B] and signifies the old ways—the original, biblical, timeless Truths.[C]

Stand at the crossroads and look;
ask for the ancient paths,
ask where the good way is, and walk in it,
and you will find rest for your souls.
Jeremiah 6:16

The world today believes truth is relative, but that's wrong. Truth is absolute and anchored in Scripture. If God's Truth is abandoned, walls crumble, and the enemy gains access to our soul. God's Truth will never change.

This gate was close to a corner of the wall. A corner provides stability and security to the entire structure. Christ is the chief cornerstone[4] of our lives.

The Valley Gate

The Valley Gate was repaired by Hanun…
They rebuilt it and put its doors and bolts and bars in place.[5]

There is a long distance before you come to this gate which opens to the Valley of Hinnom.^C

Sooner or later, the valleys of life (trials) will come. Christ guaranteed it.[6] It is during these times God grows us to be more like Jesus (sanctification) so we can reflect His perfect grace. We must prioritize the holiness of our churches and keep them pure, free from worldly values. Not much grows on mountaintops, but valleys are lush with growth. Likewise, our spiritual lives flourish and produce fruit in the valley—during our suffering and challenges.

The Dung Gate

The Dung Gate was repaired by Malkijah son of Recab…
He rebuilt it and put its
doors and bolts and bars in place. [7]

———

There is a long distance to The Dung Gate, suggesting the valley experience can go on for some time. The people took all the garbage and animal dung out of Jerusalem through The Dung Gate, down to the Valley of Hinnom to be burned by fire^C (the place where Judah sacrificed their children to Molech).[8]

Every day the world offers us garbage, tempting us with sin. Instead of throwing it out, we allow it to take root! We must get rid of what defiles us or it may destroy us.

> Let us purify ourselves from everything
> that contaminates body and spirit.
> 2 Corinthians 7:1

Our suffering and trials refine our faith by fire and produce spiritual fruit. As we humbly yield to God in repentance, He cleanses and purifies us from our sins.

Up to now, we have been moving downward and the experiences have been hard, but now there is a sharp turn in the wall, and we begin to move back upward.

The Fountain Gate

The Fountain Gate was repaired by Shallun son of Kol-Hozeh...
He rebuilt it, roofing it over and
putting its doors and bolts and bars in place. [9]

Extremely close to the Dung Gate,[C] the Fountain Gate was at the end of the Pool of Siloam.[B] It was the primary access to the fountain, the Gihon Spring, from which the city of Jerusalem received its fresh water supply.

After a valley experience when God cleans out the garbage (sin) that clogs our lives, fountains of living water (representing the Holy Spirit) begin to flow, cleansing and strengthening us to live righteously for Jesus. We are to ask the Holy Spirit to fill us daily and rivers of living spiritual water will flow from our hearts.

Whoever believes in me, as the Scripture has said,
streams of living water will flow from within him.
John 7:38

The Water Gate

The temple servants living on the hill of Ophel made repairs
up to a point opposite the Water Gate
toward the east and the projecting tower. [10]

The Water Gate was beside the Fountain Gate,[C] at the beginning of Hezekiah's tunnel and Gihon Spring. (Hezekiah built an underground tunnel to bring the spring's waters into the city.[D] It flows from The Fountain Gate to the Water Gate. It's still there.) Water is a symbol of God's Word; Jesus referred to Himself as Living Water.[11] His Word waters our thirsty souls and is our source of strength.

Ezra opened the Book of the Law of Moses at this gate[12] and read the Torah to the Jews. We must wash daily in God's Word to prepare for the trials to come. The Holy Spirit makes God's Word come alive with understanding.

Note: this gate didn't need repair—just the walls adjacent to it; it was in the only part of the wall still standing. God's Word never breaks down, needs repair or improvement; it is everlasting and perfect.

> No word from God will ever fail.
> Luke 1:37

The Horse Gate

Above the Horse Gate, the priests made repairs,
each in front of his own house. [13]

———

Through this gate, horses entered and exited the palace grounds.[B] In those days, horses had one purpose: battle. They were used to pull chariots and carry soldiers mounted for the cavalry. Horses are a symbol of war.[B]

All Christians face spiritual battles. The Horse Gate follows The Water (Word) Gate. God's Word is our sword, our offensive weapon in spiritual battles. We must always be ready to defend ourselves when attacked.

This gate and the next two gates prophesy the return of Jesus Christ. The Horse Gate reminds us of Jesus coming on a white horse at the end time judgment. All three are very close together, as are the events which they symbolize.

I saw heaven standing open
and there before me was a white horse,
whose rider is called Faithful and True.
With justice he judges and makes war.
Revelation 19:11

The East Gate

Shemaiah son of Shecaniah,
the guard at the East Gate, made repairs. [14]

The East Gate (now called The Golden Gate) is the oldest gate[E] and faces the Mount of Olives.[C] It was the main entrance to the Temple.[B] It faces east and is the gate through which Jesus humbly entered on a donkey on Palm Sunday.[E] When Jesus returns, the Bible says He will enter the Temple through this gate for His thousand-year reign.

The glory of the Lord entered the temple
through the gate facing east.
Ezekiel 43:4

bb

Muslims filled in this gate in A.D. 1530 with massive stone masonry.ᴱ Ezekiel prophesied that "a gate facing east" would be sealed. This is the only gate that is sealed.

The LORD said to me, "This gate is
to remain shut. It must not be opened."
Ezekiel 44:2

They built a cemetery in front of it to prevent Jesus's return by blocking the entrance.ᴱ If the sealed gate wouldn't stop Him, the cemetery would. (Jesus, as a Jew, would become unclean if he touched anything associated with death.) Even the Muslims understood the prophesy from Ezekiel and strategized to prevent Jesus from entering it.

cc

The Inspection Gate

Malkijah…made repairs as far as the house of the temple servants and the merchants, opposite the Inspection Gate. [15]

This final gate is also called The Gate of Judgment. The priest took the body of the animal sacrificed as a sin offering through this gate to the place for burning and disposal.[F] The elders sat at this gate judging and deciding disputes.[B] It prophecies the Judgment Seat of Christ.

When Jesus returns, there will be two judgments.

- The unsaved will appear before the *thronos* where they will be judged regarding salvation.
- Believers will appear before the *bema* where their works will be judged and rewards handed out.[16]

All our works will be tried by fire to determine their eternal value.[17]

The Sheep Gate

...between the room above the corner and the Sheep Gate the goldsmiths and merchants made repairs. [18]

Back to The Sheep Gate (now called St. Stephen's Gate or The Lion Gate). The work begins and ends here. As we come full circle, we remember our Christian walk begins and ends with Jesus and His sacrifice on the cross for our sins. Jesus is "the alpha and the omega...the beginning and the end."[19]

Note: At every gate they hung the doors and put bolts and locks in place—except this one. Any sinner can freely enter through this gate and have their sins forgiven. God won't turn anyone away; salvation is a free gift. Curiously, this is a narrow gate, compared to the others.

Narrow is the gate and difficult is the way which
leads to life, and there are few who find it.
Matthew 7:14, NKJV

dd

Jesus said, "…
I am the gate for the sheep…
whoever enters through me will be saved."
John 10:7, 9

Application:

The Church is broken because we have become careless about the condition of the gates and walls of our spiritual lives, which lie in piles of rubble.

- We need to return to the basics—back to the Gospel. (THE SHEEP GATE)

- Then we go fishing. We must ask Jesus into our boat; here He will show us where to cast our nets and guide us in evangelism. (THE FISH GATE)

- We must adhere to the right foundation—our cornerstone—for stability. And build our lives on God's Truth, which never changes. (THE OLD GATE)

- We should be aware of the true condition of the Church. There's a lot of sinful, worldly practices in our churches, such as New Age, pantheism, and tolerance over God's Truth.
  (THE VALLEY GATE)

- We must get rid of the sin and garbage in our lives that are clogging up the system before the water can flow again. Humility and repentance are key.
  (THE DUNG GATE)

- When the Living Water of the Holy Spirit is once again flowing, we will be a Spirit-filled Church.
  (THE FOUNTAIN GATE)

- It's crucial we listen to the Word of God, study it, submit to its authority, and apply it to our lives.
  (THE WATER GATE)

- Then we hitch our horses to the chariots and go to war, equipped for battle in the armor of God as we take on the forces of darkness.
  (THE HORSE GATE)

- As we battle, we continually look forward to Christ's return.
  (THE EAST GATE)

- We need never fear His judgment.
  (THE INSPECTION GATE)

- What peace to know we are saved forever.
  (THE SHEEP GATE)

Many lives lie in ruin, the result of temptation that invaded through a crumbling gate. Wrong decisions and their consequences have taken their toll. Sometimes a life needs to be knocked down and rebuilt by God's grace. God is in the restoration business. He wants to work with us to rebuild our lives—our families—our churches.

For His glory.

Jesus said, "I will build my Church
and the gates of hell
shall not prevail against it."
Matthew 16:18, ESV

How are your walls—the ones around your spiritual life that protect and defend you? Are they strong and fortified—impenetrable? Or are they crumbling from neglect? Is there a clear distinction between the way you live and the way the world lives? Are your goals, attitudes, and morals different from those around you?

Look closely because the breakdown begins slowly. First a loose piece of stone or mortar. Next, a crack in the wall. And the enemy gains access to our lives! The wall starts to crumble. Soon we lie in ruin because of sin. We are broken people living broken lives in a broken world. And unlike the walls of Jerusalem, no ordinary man can put us and our walls back together again—only an extraordinary Man named Jesus Christ. Through the Holy Spirit, He can rebuild our walls and work on the reconstruction needed within.

[1] Nehemiah 3:1

[2] Nehemiah 3:3

[3] Nehemiah 3:6

[4] Ephesians 2:20

[5] Nehemiah 3:13

[6] John 16:33a – In this world you will have trouble.

[7] Nehemiah 3:14

[8] 2 Kings 23:10

[9] Nehemiah 3:15

[10] Nehemiah 3:26

[11] Jeremiah 2:13a – They have forsaken me, the spring of living water.

[12] Nehemiah 8:1

[13] Nehemiah 3:28

[14] Nehemiah 3:29b

[15] Nehemiah 3:31

[16] 1 Corinthians 3:8 – They will…be rewarded according to their own labor.

[17] 1 Corinthians 3:13 – Their work will be…revealed with fire.

[18] Nehemiah 3:32

[19] Revelation 22:13

30

The Sacred Invades the Secular

He dismissed the crowd.
Matthew 14:22b

*I*t happened right after the feeding of the 5000 (which many scholars believe was closer to at least 10,000—maybe as many as 20,000 in total—with women and children included). Regardless, the crowd was substantial! The people were clamoring around Jesus with so many needs, yet He sent them on their way. This seems shocking!

After he had dismissed them,
he went up on a mountainside
by himself to pray.
Matthew 14:23a

Was this rude? Insensitive? Let's peek in for a closer look.

Earlier in the day, out of great compassion, Jesus healed many in the crowd before He fed them. But the day was drawing to a close and Jesus needed to spend time with His Father.

One of the most remarkable things in Scripture is how much time Jesus spent in prayer. He only had three years of public ministry, yet He was never too busy for prayer. Why? Because it was essential! In fact, according to Dr. Dan

Crawford, professor at Southwestern Seminary, the most widely used verb throughout Jesus's ministry was the verb, "to pray." Not including the Psalms, which is a prayer book of its own, the Bible records over 650 prayers, 450 of which have recorded answers. Prayer was, and continues to be, a very important spiritual discipline.

Jesus often made deliberate choices to prioritize the best. He frequently rose early to spend time with His Father.

> Very early in the morning,
> while it was still dark,
> Jesus got up, left the house and went off
> to a solitary place, where he prayed.
> Mark 1:35

Jesus also spent entire nights in prayer. Whatever the cost, unhurried prayer was a priority. This was how He handled stress, balanced His numerous responsibilities, and distinguished between worldly distractions and divine appointments. According to Dr. Charles Stanley, prayer "was Jesus's source of power, energy, and wisdom. Therefore, it was the wisest use of His time." No one could have been busier than Jesus, but he was never too busy to pray. Martin Luther once remarked, "I have so much to do that I shall spend the first three hours in prayer."

Our need to pray

How quickly and haphazardly, by contrast, we pray.

Life can be hard; there's no denying it. Trying to live the Christian life in our own strength is exhausting; serving and giving to others is draining. We often come away feeling defeated. God knows we only have so much energy. We need time to rest. We need His strength. If the Son of God felt the need to be in constant communion with His Father in Heaven, how much more should we?

Abraham Lincoln understood this well: "I have been driven many times to my knees by the overwhelming conviction that I had nowhere else to go." The Bible promises, "The prayer of a righteous person is powerful and effective."[1] Our prayers matter! God is honored when we pray.

When speaking with His disciples one day, Jesus said,

> "I will do whatever you ask in my name,
> so that the Father may be glorified in the Son."
> John 14:13

Note the key words: **in my name**.

Jesus is clear: when we pray *in Jesus's name*, we are really telling the Father, "For Your glory!" What a beautiful and easy way to glorify God!

Prayer is a privilege

In the Old Testament, the average person couldn't pray directly to God; they were too sinful to come before His holiness which is what necessitated so many animal sacrifices. Jesus died to break down the barrier between sinful people and holy God. He made us priests, granting us full access to our Father by the blood of Christ.

"Prayer," declared Oswald Chambers, "is coming into perfect fellowship and oneness with God."[A] What an incredible privilege! No wonder Jesus told us to be devoted to prayer.[2] David Jeremiah claimed, "Prayer is the highest and holiest work to which man can rise."

Prayer is unnatural

Prayer is a spiritual discipline, yet it doesn't come naturally. We all encounter obstacles to praying: finding the time, having the energy, fighting distractions, not knowing what to pray, etc. Satan and his minions dance with glee when they can keep us from praying and fostering this vital connection with God.

Our prayers are a direct line to Heaven—to the throne of the Creator of the universe. The line is always open; it's never busy.

> Let us…approach God's throne of grace
> with confidence, so that we may receive mercy
> and find grace to help us in our time of need.
> Hebrews 4:16

How should we pray?

Here is a simple acronym I find useful: ACTS.

- A=Adoration
  Praise God for who He is.
- C=Confession
  Confess your sins, repent (express regret), and ask for forgiveness. (Unconfessed sins can hinder prayers by putting a wedge between you and God.)
- T=Thanksgiving
  Thank God for all He does for you.
- S=Supplication
  Ask God to supply your needs and desires, as well as those of others.

Our prayers can be simple. Jesus's recorded prayers are surprisingly brief. Our prayers need not be long, nor eloquent. Approach God with a heart of humility, acknowledging He is in control. This posture glorifies Him.

Some things won't happen unless we pray. James tells us, "You do not have because you do not ask God."[3] Prayer can make a difference in what happens in our lives. Keep praying and don't lose heart. God is listening.

We cannot surprise God or drive Him away with our prayers. Nothing is too insignificant for God, nor too big for Him to handle. The Holy Spirit knows our heart and mind. He hears our prayers and aligns them with God's will, filling in words when we cannot.

Let's not be afraid to pray, "Not my will, but yours be done," as Jesus prayed, just before the cross.[4] God lives outside of time; He lives in our present, yet He is also already in our future. He knows the end point of our prayers—where they will take us. Since our human understanding is so limited, it is wisest if we ask Him not to do anything outside of His perfect will, but to do what's best. Even if it means overriding our desires. Perhaps He has a different trajectory for our lives that will work out even better than what we pray for. "Nothing lies beyond the reach of prayer," states Preacher Phillips Brooks, "except that which lies outside the will of God."

Do your prayers focus mainly on what you desire from God or what God desires for you? His will or your will?

Paul tells us to "Pray continually."[5] Continual prayer occurs as we walk with the Holy Spirit; it is a posture of being mindful of the presence of God—living in unbroken dependence on Him—as we communicate with Him throughout the day. Mother Teresa recognized, "Prayer is the breath of life to our soul." When asked, "What's more important: prayer or reading the Bible?" Preacher Charles

Spurgeon replied, "What is more important: breathing in or breathing out?" Does prayer permeate all you do?

God listens intently to our prayers and our words ignite His power! Priscilla Shirer asserts, "Prayer is the portal that brings the power of Heaven down to Earth."[3] When we pray, the sacred invades the secular. Prayer is our most powerful weapon as we battle day to day!

Author Lettie Burd Cowman painted a powerful picture when she said, "As a sound may dislodge an avalanche, so the prayer of faith sets in motion the power of God." The joy we feel when we engage with the One who cherishes nothing more than spending time with us is truly profound. Failing to pray means severing our essential lifeline to God.

God adores you

Don't overlook this vital spiritual discipline. Christians *must* pray. Martin Luther warned, "To be a Christian without prayer is no more possible than to be alive without breathing." Nurture and cherish this critical connection with your Creator. Treasure this privilege; don't take it lightly!

God treasures you and yearns to hear from you!

---

[1] James 5:16b

[2] Romans 12:12 – Be…faithful in prayer.

[3] James 4:2

[4] Luke 22:42 – Father, if you are willing, take this cup from me; yet not my will, but yours be done.

[5] 1 Thessalonians 5:17

31

Answered Prayer

*H*ave you ever heard people say things like this?

- "Thanks for your prayers. They worked!"
- "Keep praying; they're working!"

I know what they mean; their prayers are being answered in the way they wanted. But is this biblical?[1]

Let's step back and take a closer look. First, the purpose of prayer is this: to glorify God. It is the primary way we grow in our relationship and draw near to Him.

As we approach Him in humility and submit to His authority, He brings our will into alignment with His. If we're being completely honest, most of our prayers seek our personal comfort, success, and pleasure over God's glory. It's only human, but we need to be aware of this tendency.

How does God answer prayer?

Many of us pray, then immediately move on. But it's important to remember that talking to God is only half of prayer. Listening for His answer is the other crucial half. Be quiet before Him, fully engaged to hear His voice from His throne of endless glory. The more we know Jesus, the more we will recognize His voice when He speaks.

My soul is quiet and waits for God alone.
My hope comes from Him.
Psalm 62:5, NLV

It requires disciplined stillness to wait patiently and expectantly, eagerly anticipating His answer. When God speaks, we are on holy ground! What a profound blessing! The Creator of the universe communicates directly with us—His children. Let's not be so busy that we miss His answers. Does He get a busy signal when He tries to get through to you?

Be still before the Lord and
wait patiently for him.
Psalm 37:7a

Today, God primarily speaks through His Word, which is why it's important to read the Bible every day. In addition, the Holy Spirit offers us inaudible, yet distinct promptings in our stillness of spirit.

I most often hear answers to prayer in the quiet solitude of the early morning hours—when I am just waking up yet am not fully awake and engaged. I receive unmistakable clarity in situations where I have been seeking guidance or wisdom. God also speaks through other people: sermons, podcasts, lectures, or daily conversations.

God will answer prayer in one of three ways:
1. Yes
2. No; I have something better planned for you.
3. Not yet.

Sometimes God answers "Yes"

This is when we're tempted to say, "Prayer worked." It implies God did what we wanted. The problem is that this infers we are so powerful we can make God do what we want simply by treating Him as a vending machine. This is not biblical.

Sometimes God answers "No"

The natural response is to conclude that prayer didn't work. This reduces the value of prayer to its efficacy as we judge it. We tell ourselves, "Prayer must be useless" and it quickly loses its appeal.

This is convoluted—we are focusing on our prayer when we should be focusing on God. Regardless of our impression, God is always working in our lives to bring about His greater purposes and to achieve His will.

Prayer shouldn't be used to try to change God or get Him to give us what we want. If we think prayer is intended to give us everything we ask for, we have misunderstood the point. Whether or not God answers our prayers the way we want, all prayers "work."

C.S. Lewis stated, "Prayer doesn't change God, it changes me." The more we pray, the more we become like Jesus. If God didn't change our circumstances through our prayers, perhaps He is changing us.

If He answers, "No," then He has something a whole lot better in mind for us—from an eternal perspective.

What if we are met with silence?

Sometimes God doesn't answer our prayers right away and we are tempted to think our prayers aren't working. His answer may take a while…years or decades even. It is so hard to be met with silence. If there is a delay in His answer, know it is for a reason.

> Let all that I am
> wait quietly before God.
> Psalm 62:5a, NLT

God hears every prayer; His silence will not last forever. Although we are most concerned about our physical and immediate needs, God is most concerned about our spiritual and eternal welfare. What is difficult now may be the best thing for eternity. In His perfect timing, His answer will come. As we wait with hopeful expectation, we trust His timing. God's got it under control.

Our current situation always seems extremely important and urgent. Many times, we feel there is no way out of the crisis. Anxiety mounts and worries explode. Anxiety is an expensive and self-destructive habit. Maybe it would be worth the cost if it worked, but it doesn't. It's futile. It has never lightened a load; instead, it ruins lives.

What we sometimes forget

There is always a spiritual reality associated with our earthly one—a whole unseen world we can't appreciate until we reach Heaven. But God can. If He delays His answer, there's good reason; we must trust Him in what we cannot see. God's word assures us He is always in control.

> [He] is able to do far more abundantly
> beyond all that we ask or think.
> Ephesians 3:20a, NASB (brackets mine)

God always answers prayer. Even if He doesn't answer in the way we want or the timing we expect, He is still a good God. Elisabeth Elliot, author and missionary, once said, "Things happen which would not happen without prayer. Let us not forget that."

Prayer always "works." When He answers our prayers, the Holy Spirit instills hope where there is none, lavishes us with His peace to eliminate our anxieties, strengthens us to carry out His will despite our weaknesses, and rejuvenates our spirits.

---

[1] James 4:8, ESV – Draw near to God, and he will draw near to you.

32

Lakes and Creeks

During a leisurely stroll one autumn day, I stumbled upon a stunning lake. It was a serene and breathtaking scene. The sky was a deep expanse of blue merriment dappled with puffy white clouds dancing gracefully overhead. The lake was rimmed with aspen trees displaying their golden magnificence while maples blazed with crimson beauty. It was a sight to behold, yet what truly took my breath away was the flawless reflection of these trees on the water's surface. It was crystal clear, not a single ripple to distort the image.

I couldn't resist sitting down to immerse myself in the splendor of God's creation—His glory on full display. What a precious gift from Him meant specifically for me in that moment. I could hardly take it in.

Another day, I set out on a peaceful hike through the majestic North Carolina mountains. I stumbled upon a charming creek coursing through the rocky terrain, gracefully winding its way among the trees and crags. The water flowed freely, brimming with vitality.

Much of the time, we resemble the creek, coursing through life, maneuvering skillfully around and over rocky challenges and obstacles, moving quickly onto the next pursuit. We go many places and see countless things. We thrive on staying busy; being always on the move is deeply ingrained.

Yet I wonder...

Lakes and creeks—both beautiful in their own unique way. Yet I wonder if perhaps our true nature—the way we were created and should aspire to be—aligns better with that of a lake. Unlike creeks and rivers which move continually, lakes embrace serenity and stillness, allowing for beautiful reflections—something of which moving waters are incapable.

God desires that we not settle for superficial relationships with Him or others, but instead pursue and embrace the riches of profound and meaningful connections—akin to deep lakes.

As we are still before Him, the whirlwind of busyness quieted down, we have time to seek the restorative nature of His presence. And He rewards us with His abiding peace and tranquility. Much like the lake's surface, we respond by naturally reflecting the beauty of His character and holiness—His dazzling glory!

33

Loving Porcupine People

*P*orcupine people. We all have them in our lives. Difficult people who are prickly to be around.

- Possibly a parent who criticizes you repeatedly and can't find much good in what you do.
- Maybe a friend whose loyalty is questionable.
- A co-worker who continually gets on your nerves.
- Perhaps an adult child who has turned against you.

I'm betting you have tried to do the right thing—to calm the waters with little to no success. Being around porcupine people is exhausting and depleting.

Who are porcupine people?

Let's back up a moment and define porcupine people. These individuals have an overabundance of self-righteous attitude. Most lack healthy self-esteem, so to compensate, they tend to seek value by belittling others. Sarcasm, ridicule, and passive-aggressive behavior are common weapons of this disagreeable personality. They may lie, spread rumors, and try to manipulate people. They take advantage of the kindness and generosity of others and will consume their time and energy without regard. They are usually very unhappy—utterly miserable—yet seem relatively content on the surface.

In nature, a porcupine will run backward to force its quills into a predator. Similarly, human porcupines can also inflict pain—emotional pain. However, they may not necessarily be trying to hurt others and may even be oblivious to their subconscious defense mechanisms. How should you respond when you fall victim to such a person?

Look up

Prayer is essential; you need divine guidance on how to deal with this person and find peace. Instead of talking with other people about your porcupine, talk with God. He sees the whole picture, including why this person acts as he does. He knows the reason behind your porcupine's actions and is the only One who can guide and support you perfectly. Allow Him to direct your steps.

Look in

God has allowed this person into your life for some reason. What is God showing you about yourself through your interactions with this prickly person? Perhaps He is using this relationship to refine you—to make you more like Jesus.

Look out

Look beyond the quills to see the person within. Many porcupine people have suffered physical or emotional trauma triggering insecurities, causing them to erect barriers to protect themselves. Most have been hurt. You may never know what has happened to this person to cause them to be the person they are today. Pray for them.

Regardless, at some point you will have to interact with and respond to them.

Moses offers great advice:

> You must be blameless
> before the Lord your God.
> Deuteronomy 18:13

Always do your best to respond in such a way that you can't be blamed for anything later on. Seek to become as blameless as possible. Imagine being in a courtroom. You're in the hot seat and the judge lowers his gavel and announces, "Court is in session." The plaintiff's attorney asks you if you have ever said or done anything that could be *perceived* as offensive to his client. Would you be found guilty? "Blessed are those whose ways are blameless."[1]

> Let God weigh me in
> honest scales and he will know
> that I am blameless.
> Job 31:6

Do not allow the enemy to tempt you to retaliate or respond in kind to their brash behavior. Don't allow your wounds to turn you into someone you are not. It's not worth compromising your integrity and witness by sinking to their level. Rise above it. As they later reflect upon their interaction with you, the last thing you want is for them to judge something you said or did as justification for their actions.

> Do not repay anyone evil for evil.
> Be careful to do what is right
> in the eyes of everybody.
> Romans 12:17

When they hurt you, it's ok to respectfully tell them how their words or actions are damaging. Pray for understanding and repentance from your porcupine person.

However, it's not your job to fix other people; that's God's job. Your job is to forgive and offer grace, even when it's hard and undeserved. God has extended unmerited grace to us more times than we can count! We are to do the same as we love others with humility the way Christ loves us. Choose a gentle response which will engender peace.[2]

Toxic people

There are other people I call toxic. They are porcupine people ramped up a few notches—very negative, controlling, manipulative, and selfish. Every conversation is always all about them. They can be cold and abrasive. They judge harshly and have a short temper, taking out their frustrations on those with milder temperaments. They may go into attack mode. Toxic people cause others considerable anxiety and stress.

It is highly unlikely a toxic person will change, except by the grace of God. It's best to minimize their involvement in your life and love them from afar. The Bible addresses this type of person.

> Their venom is like
> the venom of a snake.
> Psalm 58:4a

They are emotionally poisonous. An older relative was toxic to me for many years. She alienated everyone in her life with highly critical and controlling actions such that in her later years, I was all she had left. Even paid help never stayed long. It took years, but I learned to set strong boundaries and refused to be manipulated by her. She berated my family repeatedly, relatives long dead, and made up lies specifically to hurt me. I recoiled more times than I can count. Yet she called me relentlessly with selfish, demanding requests, often as many as eight times/day. A wise person cautioned, "Be careful what you tolerate. You are teaching people how to treat you."

Whether your toxic person is a relative or not, you must set firm boundaries and adhere to them. Your life presents its own set of life challenges and priorities without being consumed by this person's issues and demands. Assert your position respectfully, yet firmly.

> "Show respect to people who don't even deserve it;
> not as a reflection of their character,
> but as a reflection of yours."[A]
> Pastor Dave Willis

Seek peace, if possible, and do not allow the behavior of others to destroy your inner peace.

> If it is possible, as far as it depends on you,
> live at peace with everyone.
> Romans 12:18

Sometimes peace cannot be achieved. If the stress of being with this person sends your emotions reeling, controls you, robs you of His peace, drains your time and energies, hurts your family, or impacts your health, pray for God to erect a hedge of protection around you.

You may come to a point where you need to cut them out of your life completely. You are not at the mercy of this person. As you prayerfully seek God's wisdom, He will guide you through this decision and speak peace to your soul, affirming the direction you are to take. Above all, God seeks your holiness as you reflect His glory when you deal with difficult people.

> May he strengthen your hearts
> so that you will be blameless and holy
> in the presence of our God and Father.
> 1 Thessalonians 3:13

May the Lord bless you and watch over you as you glorify Him in dealing with your porcupine person. May you never forget to seek and gather His divine manna to enrich and nourish your soul as He provides exactly what you need each day, in a way only He can.

His grace will be sufficient.

One final tough consideration

If you find yourself around countless porcupine people everywhere you go, perhaps look to see if you've sprouted quills! It's possible you have become the porcupine. Seek God's face for guidance in turning yourself around.

---

[1] Psalm 119:1a

[2] Proverbs 15:1a – A gentle answer turns away wrath.

34

Slaves to Sin

*L*ucifer started it all! He was an angel, in fact the most beautiful and powerful of all the angels. Oh, how his head swelled with pride! He longed to be more powerful than God; he wanted to be God. Because of his pride, he was cast out of Heaven. We now call him Satan.

Satan spends his time wielding his power by creating chaos. Because of his hatred for God, he brought sin into His creation when he lured Adam and Eve with the temptation to be like God. Adam and Eve made a deadly choice. They rejected God's glory and chose to yield to temptation. When they sinned, Satan unleashed evil; sin and death let loose, invading the human race and all of creation.[1] The whole world was impacted! And the inner nature of mankind suffered a radical transformation. Adam and Eve now had a sin nature which has been passed on to every human being since that time.

In essence, sin is now an integral part of our spiritual DNA. Because of our sin nature, we struggle with sin every day. We aren't sinners because we sin; we sin because have a sin nature. Sin is rooted in us… in our pride. It is self-seeking, self-focused, and self-indulgent. Yet, because of God's indelible imprint on our soul, we never really feel right when we do what is wrong. This leads to unrest and lack of peace as we find ourselves in the murky pit of sin's filth. Sin always promises more than it can deliver. The initial enjoyment is soon gone, and we are trapped, its hold on us far more powerful than we could have imagined.

- ## Sin is deceptive.

     We think the world offers something God can't or won't give us. Sin looks so attractive that we begin to think we will be unhappy without it. It lures us in by making us think the thrill of indulging is grand! We pursue it at all costs, believing it will bring joy. It almost always starts out as fun. It feels good for a time—the temporary high of going somewhere we shouldn't go, the buzz of a drug or drink we should stay away from, the secret pleasure of looking at something online we shouldn't see, the thrill of a hook-up. But the initial pleasure is short-lived with no lasting depth. We quickly find it wasn't what it claimed to be. "Sin constantly invites us to sacrifice a greater reward by choosing a lesser thrill that always fails to deliver what it promises."[A]

     Widely acclaimed entrepreneurs and bestselling authors David and Jason Benham warn, "God's blessings are found inside God's boundaries. If you go outside his boundaries, His blessings are replaced with burdens." There is good reason we have boundaries.

     We rationalize our choices, telling ourselves times have changed and what used to be sin is sin no longer. Sin blinds our hearts to the truth. If the Bible calls it sin, our opinion doesn't matter. God is unchanging. Our rationalizations do not hold up in the face of God's everlasting holiness.

     Too often, we let our guard down, becoming unsuspecting and falling prey to the deceptions of Satan. One day, my husband dropped me off at a mega mall for a quick return. As I ran inside, the sky opened, sending down rain in torrents! Bob drove off in his gray Honda Accord to circle back and pick me up ten minutes later.

My return was quick, and I hurried to the exit. Rain was pelting and dense, causing terrible visibility as it pounded mercilessly all around. When I saw the gray car pull up, I ran out as fast as I could, opened the passenger door and threw myself into the front seat, dripping wet! After a moment, I turned to look at Bob, only to set my eyes on a strange man with eyes bugging out of his head. Of course, I asked the obvious! "What are you doing in our car?" He just stammered.

Meanwhile, Bob, two cars back, was watching the entire scene unfold. Humored, I'm sure he was thinking, *Let's see how long this lasts. He will soon realize how high maintenance she is and return her in no time flat!*

Sure enough!

"I'm in the wrong car, aren't I?" He nodded. I apologized and shot out of that car like a torpedo! I looked up in time to see his wife running to their car, looking very confused! *Let him explain that one,* I thought!

There are a lot of gray sedans in the world! They all look alike, especially in a blinding storm. Satan will send any number of gray sedans to pick you up and take you where you don't want to go. Make sure you pay attention and know who is driving. Be discerning! Is God navigating your course? Or someone less trustworthy? Who do you trust with your soul?

- **Sin is addictive.**

    Every sin begins with a step onto a path that leads somewhere. We often take that first step because we are curious, or it sounds exciting and fun, but we rarely look down that path to see where it leads. No one ever said,

➤ "One day I hope to become an alcoholic."
➤ "I hope to get pregnant as an unmarried teen."
➤ "I hope to be in tremendous, crippling debt."

Every time we sin, we desensitize ourselves just a bit, reinforcing a pattern that becomes harder to break each time we transgress. It's addictive! The endless desire for a greater thrill leads to more sin. Before we know it, we're well down a destructive path and can't find our way back. In a sermon, Pastor Joe Brown preached, "Humans are the only species that runs faster when they're lost." Running away from our problems is a race we'll never win! We have become slaves to our sin.[2]

Sometimes the addictive sin *seems* less bad, like the addiction to social media, shopping, exercise, smart phones, or TV. As one example, let's consider video game addiction. The Addiction Center states, "Video games affect the brain in the same way as addictive drugs; they trigger the release of Dopamine, a chemical which reinforces behavior."[B] Don't be fooled; no sin is less bad. All sin is destructive.

> You are a slave to whatever controls you.
> 2 Peter 2:19b, NLT

Freedom isn't doing anything we want. By doing what feels good or sounds exciting (with no moral compass), we end up becoming slaves to what our bodies want. Our desire has become our master.

Bertrand Russell, an 18th century philosopher, remarked, "The chains of habit are too light to be felt until they are too heavy to be broken."[C]

> As a dog returns to its vomit,
> so fools repeat their folly.
> Proverbs 26:11

If you've ever had dogs, you know this verse to be true. It is a disgusting behavior which makes no sense to us. It's like a magnetic pull that draws the dog back. When we watch our loved ones return to their cruel masters, drawn back to the disgusting habits of their sin, it's like watching them return to devour their own vomit—as if they don't know where else to turn. Each subsequent trip offers less satisfaction yet demands a higher price. Voltaire cautioned, "It is difficult to free fools from the chains they revere." No one is immune. Each of us can be guilty of repeating the same foolish actions over and over again.

- **Sin escalates.**

  We seldom foresee sin's escalating damage when we take that first step. White lies turn into bigger lies which become a lifestyle. Anger becomes hatred, which leads to rage. Indulging in drugs leads to the desire for more and at higher dosages. Envy leads to bitterness which steals joy and hurts relationships. Lesser thrills yield to the desire for greater thrills.

- **Sin separates us from God.**

  Sin creates a void deep in our soul which swells as we try to fill it with things from this world. We ignore

God and His warnings that destruction is looming. Worldly things cannot fill the void; it can only be filled with God Himself.

> Your sins have cut you off from God.
> Isaiah 59:2a, TLB

• **Sin is destructive.**

Sin isolates. Dietrich Bonhoeffer explained, "The more isolated a person is, the more destructive will be the power of sin over him."[D] Sin can cost us valuable relationships, harm our family, destroy our bank account, hurt our career, steal our joy, and ruin our integrity. Sin quietly steals our freedoms as it hardens our hearts.

Christian apologist, Ravi Zacharias once noted, "Sin will take you farther than you want to go, keep you longer than you want to stay, and cost you more than you want to pay." Sadly, he didn't take his own warnings seriously and fell victim to his own desires of passion, hurting his family, harming numerous people, and destroying his character. Worst of all, he dishonored God and severely damaged his Christian witness. His 40-year international apologetics ministry crumbled to ashes after his death—when his hypocrisy was revealed.

Are you tired of allowing your sin and destructive habits to control you? Do you want to be free? If you answered yes, there is hope. You've just made the first step.

---

[1] Romans 5:12 – Just as sin entered the world through one man, and death through sin, and in this way death came to all people, because all sinned.

[2] John 8:34 – Jesus replied, "Everyone who sins is a slave to sin."

35

Breaking the Chains of Sin

ohn Piper once said, "Preferring anything above Christ is the very essence of sin. It must be fought."ᴬ How do we do this? Where do we even begin?

It begins with the desire to *want* to stop sinning. We must admit we have a problem, yearn to be set free, and be willing to do what it takes to be released from its grip. Sin cannot be controlled; it must be eradicated completely, or else it will harm and destroy. It will be a fight.

> Your foolish desires will destroy you…
> you must give up your old way of life
> with all its bad habits.
> Let the Spirit change your way of thinking
> and make you into a new person.
> You were created to be like God,
> and so you must please him and be truly holy.
> Ephesians 4:22-24, CEV

The world changes us from the outside in. It tells us to patch the old sinful nature, like applying a bandage, and then we're good to go! But God transforms us from the inside out by getting rid of the old self. Patching doesn't work; we need full transformation!

When we cling to sin, we lose the power, peace, and joy of the Holy Spirit. Oswald Chambers sums it up well:

"If sin rules in me,
God's life in me will be killed;
if God rules in me, sin in me will be killed.
There is nothing more fundamental than that."[B]

Freedom is possible

We must choose our master. Either we are slaves to sin—and not free. Or with God as our master, we can find freedom—true freedom—from sin and our past.

First, we must want to be free. Some of us want to give up instead. We fear we have ruined God's plan for our lives with our own mistakes. If this is you, relax! You're not that powerful! Yet God is more than capable of freeing you.

Second, we must take that first step of seeking God through prayer. God "commands all people everywhere to repent."[1] *Repent* is not just an apology. It means an about face—a 180° turnaround from one way of life to another—from sin to God.[C] When we repent, God forgives us, then we turn from our sin to new life and freedom. In God's strength, we commit to do what it takes to overcome the hold sin has on us.

Do not let sin control the way you live;
do not give in to sinful desires.
Do not let any part of your body become
an instrument of evil to serve sin.

Instead, give yourselves completely to God,
for you were dead, but now you have new life.
So use your whole body as an instrument
to do what is right for the glory of God.
Romans 6:12-13, NLT

Some of us, at least on the surface, enjoy sin so much (or perhaps it seems too hard to change) that we justify it. We tell ourselves, "What I'm doing isn't so bad." Be careful; this is dangerous. We live in a culture where sin proudly struts down Main Street and we are expected to applaud and accept it. The world often seems offended by everything but sin. Don't get sucked into this trap.

We must reject sin. The Holy Spirit resides in us with the same power that raised Christ from the dead. Prayer is the key that releases His indwelling power to transform us from the inside out. As we turn from sin, God transforms us by renewing our mind and our heart.

> Don't copy the behavior and customs of this world,
> but let God transform you into
> a new person by changing the way you think.
> Romans 12:2a, NLT

We still may have to deal with the consequences of sin, which are never pleasant. Hang in there. God can restore what sin has destroyed, bringing beauty from the brokenness. This inward change requires humility as we align our thoughts, priorities, and goals with those of Christ by clinging to God. It means reading our Bible to learn who Christ is, obeying His commands, surrounding ourselves with Christians who are following God, going to church, and seeking Christian counsel. Here is an awesome promise:

> "If you abide in my word…you will know
> the truth, and the truth will set you free."
> So if the Son sets you free, you will be free indeed.
> John 8:31b-32, 36 ESV

This is the truth we seek. As we immerse ourselves in Christ, the truth will be revealed to us.

The great paradox of freedom in Christ

We cannot pay the penalty for our own sins; we are powerless to save ourselves from its hold on us. Jesus did what we can't do. He sacrificed His life to release us from our bondage to sin. Perhaps the greatest paradox in the history of mankind is this: *The cross—a symbol of death—has given us new life!* It makes no earthly sense. Yet its heavenly truth is absolute. Our unique bondage to Christ gives us spiritual freedom with benefits too numerous to count. Nevertheless, here are a few:

- Unconditional love from God
- Unlimited grace and mercy
- Complete forgiveness
- Holy Spirit power available to us
- Peace which surpasses understanding
- Eternal life in Paradise
- Rich spiritual inheritance
- Joy of our salvation.

As we accept this outlandish gift, our chains fall to the ground and we are spiritually, eternally free! Do not give up. You will have difficult days; press on anyway. Resist the enemy as he will do all he can to keep you enslaved to your destructive sin.

Dwell in freedom, my friend, and cherish the glory of living in abandon as God intended.

---

[1] Acts 17:30b

36

❧

Their Finest Hour

The situation was extremely grim.

It was May 1940. World War II. German forces, led by Adolph Hitler, had trapped more than 350,000 Allied troops along the northern coast of France on the beach at Dunkirk.[A] British Prime Minister Winston Churchill called this a "colossal military disaster."[B] All logic pointed to total annihilation or capture of these troops by Hitler's armies. "Many of Britain's military leaders thought it was hopeless; the war was over. The Nazi savages marching under the banner of the twisted cross would reign over Europe."[A]

In an act of calculated, hope-filled courage, a British naval officer got an idea! He cabled a distress signal to London; it contained only three words: "But if not."[C] Simple and concise, yet urgent.

If you don't understand this code, you're not alone. But in 1940, the British people immediately understood the meaning because they knew their Bible. Their army revered God and turned to Him for prayer, strength, and courage during the war.[D]

This coded message was based on Daniel and his three Jewish friends who were held captive in Babylon. Shadrach, Meshach and Abednego defied the king's edict forcing them to worship and bow down to his false gods and a golden image he had set up. The punishment for defiance was to be thrown into a fiery furnace. Shadrach, Meshach, and Abednego answered respectfully,

> Our God whom we serve
> is able to deliver us from the burning fiery furnace,
> and he will deliver us out of your hand, O king.
> But if not…we will not serve your gods
> or worship the golden image that you have set up."
> Daniel 3:16-18

In fury, the king ordered these three young Jewish men to be thrown into the burning furnace.

Operation Dynamo

The troops believed God could rescue them if He chose to. This coded message conveyed two crucial points:

- We are in immediate danger.
- Even if God chooses not to rescue us, we will not surrender to the enemy and bow down to the gods of Hitler and the Germans.

This message galvanized the British citizens and jolted them into immediate action. United, they set a courageous plan into motion to rescue the besieged troops from certain tortuous death. A fleet of 850 vessels was hastily assembled: naval destroyers, marine boats, fishing boats, pleasure craft, yachts, ferries, tugs, barges, and lifeboats.

From May 26th to June 4th, 338,226 Allied soldiers were rescued from the beaches and harbor of Dunkirk and ferried across the English Channel.[E] This daring evacuation was named *Operation Dynamo*, also known as the *Miracle of Dunkirk*.[E]   Churchill hailed this rescue a "miracle of deliverance" in his June 4th speech, "We Shall Fight on the Beaches."[B]

Can you imagine a nation so steeped in biblical knowledge that a three-word cryptic illusion could ignite such a successful, large-scale rescue mission? God was undoubtedly behind this, rewarding the people for their obedience in knowing the Bible.

What if such a message was sent over the airwaves today? How many people would "get it?" Sadly, not many; the Bible has been devalued and often discarded. Our scriptural values have become diluted.

But…God has not changed. His Word holds true.

Biblical literacy

Where do we stand as a society on biblical literacy today? According to Pew Research, almost 25% of us haven't read a book of any kind in the past year, triple the number from 1978. And biblical literacy is far worse.[F]

A 2017 Gallup poll found that 24% of Americans believe the Bible is God's Word, the lowest percentage in 40 years.[C] A LifeWay Research study found only 45% of churchgoers read the Bible more than once each week. Almost 20% say they never read the Bible.[F] If we don't read the Bible, we can't know what it says, which is why many Christians today hold unbiblical views.

The United Kingdom Bible Society surveyed British children and found they were unable to recognize common Bible stories. Almost 1 in 3 didn't know the nativity was part of the Bible and 59% didn't know the story of Jonah and the whale was in the Bible. Their parents weren't much better.

According to this survey, 30% of British parents didn't know Adam and Eve, David and Goliath, or the Good

Samaritan were in the Bible. Even worse, according to the people polled, 27% thought Superman is or might be in the Bible. More than 33% believed the same about Harry Potter with 54% believing The Hunger Games is or might be in the Bible.[F]

America doesn't fare well

This illiteracy is not for lack of access to the Bible. In 2022, 77% of U.S. adults owned a Bible,[G] yet only 39% read the Bible at least 3-4 times/year in 2022, down 11% in the last decade. Households contain an average of 4.3 Bibles.[H] Every person with a smartphone has a Bible at their fingertips, downloadable for free.

A Lifeway Research survey reveals Americans' beliefs.[I]

- Less than 47% say the Bible is completely accurate.
- 51% feel the Bible was written for each person to interpret as he or she chooses.
- 74% feel some sins aren't a big deal.
- 77% believe people must earn salvation.
- 52% say good deeds help people earn Heaven.
- 45% believe there are many ways to get to Heaven.

A George Barna poll revealed 58% don't know who preached the Sermon on the Mount; most think it was someone on horseback.[J]

In 1948, General Omar Bradley declared, "We are technological giants and moral midgets. We have discovered the mystery of the atom, but we have forgotten The Sermon on the Mount." How tragic! Biblical illiteracy is increasing at an alarming rate! But if we want to avoid sin, we must know God's Word.

I have hidden your word in my heart
that I might not sin against you.
Psalm 119:11

We can only grow in character to be like Jesus if we know Him through His Word. Only then can we reflect His purity and holiness to those ignorant of biblical truths.

Churchill referred to the *Miracle of Dunkirk* as "their finest hour."[K] God rewarded their obedience in knowing their Bible. May we strive for *our* finest hour as we step out in faith and obedience to live for and reflect His glory.

Dunkirk movie

In July 2017, Christopher Nolan directed and produced *Dunkirk*, an apocalyptic, historical war thriller depicting the Dunkirk evacuation. Nolan also wrote the narrative that realistically portrayed the Allied evacuation from three perspectives: land, sea, and air. This extremely powerful and exciting epic became the highest-grossing WWII movie in history until Christopher Nolan's Oppenheimer surpassed it in 2023.

Dunkirk received critical acclaim for its gripping storytelling, realistic portrayal of war, and innovative use of time. It amassed 34 major nominations in 2018, securing eight awards, including the prestigious title: the 2018 American Film Institute Movie of the Year.

37

From Complaining to Gratitude

The Israelites were slaves to the Egyptians for roughly 430 years. They endured cruel and merciless treatment from sunup to sundown with a cruel taskmaster over them. God had had enough. It was time. He sent Moses and his brother Aaron to free His people from the power of the pharaoh.

As they fled Egypt, the Israelites witnessed God parting the Red Sea, aiding their escape from the Egyptians who pursued them on horseback and in chariots. When they were safely across, Moses stretched out his hand over the sea which sent the water crashing back into place, killing the entire Egyptian army. The Israelites were so overwhelmed with gratitude that they sang a song to the Lord.

Three days later

The Israelites had *just* left Mt. Sinai. It had only taken three days for discontentment to fill their hearts. They started grumbling which escalated to complaining—then quickly spiraled into angry ranting.

With the miracle of the Red Sea parting a distant memory, they transformed from grateful people to selfish ingrates. In only three days! 72 hours! No longer were they happy. They didn't like the food—the water—the travel—the monotony—or each other.

A complaining spirit

It develops so gradually we rarely notice. It starts small but builds quickly. It's amazing how fast we can forget how wonderful and good God is and how much He blesses us every single day! We begin to see what we lack and focus on what we think we deserve, fostering a mindset of bitterness. This leads to a spirit of entitlement.

The world urges us to focus on ourselves. It tells us we deserve better, and things should go our way. When they don't, we become like the Israelites. We grow dissatisfied and we grumble.

- Grumbling escalates to complaining.
- Complaining quickly becomes a habit.
- Habits become who we are.

The tendency to complain is insidious

We don't see it coming. Sadly, complaining affects everyone around us. It not only brings down the mood of those within earshot, but it is contagious.

Complaining is a direct message to God that what He has given us isn't enough—we don't like what He has allowed in our lives—He's not doing His job—He's made a mistake. A complaining spirit doesn't remember all the great things God has done for us. It's a sign of ingratitude and shows a lack of faith.

Complaining is a heart issue. It shows we are developing a hard heart that doesn't trust God. This spills over to our attitudes and our actions. The Israelites craved the things of the world more than they trusted what God provided.

Complaining is contagious; it spreads like wildfire, planting seeds of negativity and discord among those around us. It infected Moses who began complaining too, but he reacted differently than the people. He took His complaints to God, and when he did, God heard and answered him. When we cry out to God, He listens and restores our souls. He always provides exactly what we need.

> God is filled with mercy.
> his mercies are endless—new every morning.
> Lamentations 3:22b-23a, my version

The word *mercy* comes from a medieval Latin word which means "price paid." It is given by someone who has the power to punish with the connotation of choosing forgiveness, compassion, and kindness instead. The world won't extend mercy, but God is rich in mercy.[1]

Many people focus on themselves and how they can take advantage of others or a situation to get what they want. Being merciful is their last thought. Mercy comes from God; and as His disciples, we are to be full of mercy.

> Jesus taught, "Blessed are the merciful,
> for they will be shown mercy."
> Matthew 5:7

The world delights in telling us we deserve better, tempting us to focus on ourselves. When we feel we are being shortchanged, we may resort to complaining, especially when we're tired. But guess what? God drenches us in fresh mercies every morning! He never runs out. Oh, what abundance we don't deserve!

When we ask God to help us get our attitude right, gratitude fills our hearts. God pours out compassion, opening our eyes to see how much we really have—something we can't see when we complain.

It's easy to forget God is in control.

There will be times we forget. We will get sick. Kids can be a challenge. Our spouse isn't always the most attentive or understanding. Everything at home seems to break at the same time. Finances are a stress. Family doesn't understand us. Friends disappoint us. Our boss is demanding. The list goes on and on. But complaining never solves our problems.

Complaining does not reflect our good God, nor glorify Him; in fact, it dishonors Him. This negativity infects our homes. Our children may mimic and adopt this coping mechanism without realizing it. Complaining people are not happy people. It's not the legacy we want to leave behind.

How do you cope?

When things don't go your way, do you tend to grumble? What does it take to appease you? How much would others say you complain?

May the Holy Spirit grow within us a forgiving spirit of gratitude and soften our hearts to trust God with exactly what He has given us. Each day is a fresh beginning—a chance to start again. God's mercies are new every morning!

Incidentally, if the Israelites had been faithful, they could have made the journey from Egypt to the Promised Land in only eleven days, not forty years! They had much to learn in the desert—and were slow to do so!

Our faithfulness to God and the gratitude (or lack thereof) in our hearts yield consequences.

---

[1] Ephesians 2:4a, TLB – God is so rich in mercy.

38

❧

Encountering Divine Holiness

inally! The Israelites made it to the Promised Land, but it wasn't just handed to them. They had to fight many hostile groups to claim it. Having just lost a big battle, the Israelites faced more warfare. Their formidable opponent—the dreaded Philistines—posed an even greater threat. The Israelites decided to carry the Ark of the Covenant, the most sacred treasure of Israel, onto the battlefield to help them gain the victory. Tragically, they were defeated, and the Ark was captured. The people mourned! "The glory has departed from Israel for the ark of God has been captured."[1] And indeed it had, as the Ark contained the glory of God. Upon hearing the news, Eli the priest fell over dead in heartbroken despair.[2]

With the Ark in their possession, the Philistines traveled to several cities, but wherever the Ark went, disaster struck as they fell under God's curses. After seven months, they had had enough! They realized the God of Israel was indeed living and powerful; they decided it was best to return the Ark to Israel.

The Philistines hastily secured a cart, plunked the Ark on top, hitched two cows to the cart, and off they went! With a sense of relief, they delivered the Ark of the Covenant to the house of Abinadab. There it remained for twenty years, largely neglected during King Saul's reign.[3]

After Saul's death, David was crowned the second king of Israel at the age of thirty. Early in his reign, David turned his attention to the Ark of the Covenant. He sought to glorify God by returning it to Jerusalem where it belonged.

The big day!

David was so excited for this day to arrive. He gathered 30,000 carefully chosen men and planned out every detail; yet sadly, David never consulted God. Upon arriving at the house of Abinadab, they set the Ark on a simple cart and harnessed the oxen to pull it. Negotiating the descent from his hillside house with the exceptionally heavy Ark proved to be a challenging endeavor. With the Ark balanced precariously on the cart, unsecured, they started the journey.

Abinadab's two sons guided the cart with Ahio leading and Uzzah likely walking beside it. At some point, the oxen stumbled, causing the cart to teeter. Uzzah impulsively reached out to steady the Ark.

What happened next was shocking! Horrifying. Those watching were stunned. It took their breath away.

God's anger burned against Uzzah and He struck him dead on the spot![4] At first glance, this punishment appears extreme. However, God never does anything rash without good reason or thought. Let's explore further.

God had given Moses and the Israelites specific and detailed instructions about how to transport the Ark of the Covenant. It was only to be carried with great care and reverence upon the shoulders of the Levites[5] (the priestly line) using special poles inserted in rings on two sides of the Ark.[6]

No matter what, they were never to touch the Ark; doing so would result in death.[7] The Ark was also to be well covered as it represented God—His holiness—and His presence.

David and his men had carelessly imitated the manner the Philistines used to transport the Ark years earlier. They followed the pagan ways of the world which quickly led to death as God had warned. They treated the presence of God with casual regard.

That day would be forever etched in David's memory. David quickly gained a new appreciation for the awe-inspiring holiness of the Lord. We are to treat His holiness with the reverence it is due. Indifference toward His holiness (in thoughts, actions, words, and attitudes) can provoke His holy wrath.

> It is a dreadful thing to fall into
> the hands of the living God.
> Hebrews 10:31

No one wants to witness or experience God's wrath. Because of the casual way David's men handled the transport, a dangerous temptation arose they could have avoided. Because the Ark represented God's presence and glory, when Uzzah touched it, he touched the glory of God.

We are on dangerous ground when we are tempted to touch the glory of God—something which belongs only to Him. It's a great honor to serve the Lord, but the glory belongs to Him alone.

Let's reflect
We are wise to learn from the Jews, especially Uzzah.

- How often do we follow the ways of the world?
- Do we regularly consult with God?

- Where are we using a cart just because our culture does?
- Are we ever tempted to touch or grab hold of glory that belongs to God alone?

Death is a consequence of treating the holiness of God with only a careless disrespect. God expects us to know how to approach and handle what is sacred.

Here's an exciting thought

One day we may actually get a glimpse of the Ark of the Covenant as John mentions seeing the Ark in Heaven during His vision:

> Then God's temple in heaven was opened,
> and within his temple was seen
> the ark of his covenant.
> Revelation 11:19a

What a glorious day that will be!

---

[1] 1 Samuel 4:22
[2] 1 Samuel 4:3-22
[3] 1 Samuel 5:1-7:2
[4] 2 Samuel 6:1-7
[5] Numbers 7:9
[6] Exodus 25:12-14
[7] Numbers 4:15b – They must not touch the holy things or they will die.

39

Pure as Snow

We had a magnificent snowstorm this week. When the snow began to fall, I stood mesmerized as the delicate snowflakes softly floated from the heavens, graceful in their airy silence. As they gently landed, they sparkled like powdery diamond dust, tenderly blanketing our world in their crystalline perfection.

As minutes turned into hours and the hours toppled one upon the other like dominoes in a line, I watched the landscape of our common, ordinary world transform into a winter wonderland for which words were wholly inadequate. As the flakes became larger and the flurry more dense, it seemed as if we had been magically transported to a beautiful paradise, held captive by the silent embrace of icy white grandeur.

I marveled at the might of nature.

Growing up in Glendale, Wisconsin, I learned to appreciate the frequent cloudbursts of winter's greatest treat. Now that we live in the North Carolina Piedmont, snow is uncommon and an extravagant indulgence when it occurs. A certain reverence overtook me as I watched in awe of the beauty of His majesty. My soul rejoiced!

Have you ever noticed how vividly white and intensely bright freshly fallen snow is? As the sun came out, the carpet of snow shimmered as if covered with the finest gems. Nature's glory—its brilliance was almost blinding!

This verse penned by King David comes to mind:

> Cleanse me with hyssop,
> and I will be clean; wash me,
> and I will be whiter than snow.
> Psalm 51:7

Before anointing, the priests engaged in ceremonial washing practices by dipping hyssop—a shrub with hairy stems—into blood. Then they sprinkled the blood on the people, symbolizing the forgiveness of sins.

Psalm 51 is David's prayer of repentance. After being confronted with his sins of adultery and murder, he pleaded for mercy, forgiveness, and cleansing. He was drowning in guilt and shame. He deserved the death penalty. God was his only hope for redemption. Only God could purify him from his evil and sinful deeds.

David requested cleansing with hyssop, the same plant the Israelites used to dip in the lamb's blood and apply to the door frames of their homes on the very first Passover.[1] This blood saved them from certain death as they were passed over. The blood brought life.

Today we don't have such ceremonies. Instead, Jesus shed His blood on the cross to wash away our sins. When He washes us with forgiveness, Scripture tells us we are as white as snow! Forgiveness means freedom.

> Though your sins are like scarlet,
> they shall be as white as snow.
> Isaiah 1:18b

Scarlet was an intensely rich, permanent dye. The stain of sin is just as indelible to us today as the scarlet dye of Bible days.

Our minds do not forget our offenses; we replay the scenes in our heads over and over again as if they are stuck on repeat. Perhaps you feel you have been so bad there is no hope to start over. Or maybe you know someone who feels this way. We recall the people we have hurt. Regrets that torment us. Debts that hold us captive. Shame that devours us. The Lord we have betrayed. It seems the stain of sin will never go away.

It's time to quit reliving these scenes and go to the One who can remove the hideous stain. We don't have to go through life permanently blemished and soiled. When we repent, Christ forgives us and removes our most indelible stains—He paid the price on the cross. The cross is the only tool capable of defeating sin (and also death). The cross—a symbol of death, what many perceive as evil—is actually the means of our salvation from the evil of sin. His blood—and only *His* blood on the cross—has the power to cleanse us completely!

Rise above and accept this outrageous gift of forgiveness and restoration! Hurl your shame to the next county. Claim your new status as "forgiven." The stain of sin is gone! It can't be found because it wasn't simply covered up; it was erased completely. No evidence remains. You have been given a new start. Walk in this gift.

Entirely clean. No impurities. No blemishes. Spotless. Jesus alone has the power to transform you—making you shine in pristine brilliance as you reflect His glory. When our sins have been washed in the blood of Christ, we appear white as snow in the eyes of God.

We know fresh, new snow is as white at the bottom as it is at the top. Christ cleanses and purifies us with His holiness—deep down inside—through and through.

Let's rejoice in the way God has provided for our sin nature. God had a plan from before time began to restore us and redeem us in the perfect purity of Christ so we can sparkle with the beauty of His holiness.

To Him be all glory!

---

[1] Exodus 12:22 – Make a brush from a few small branches of a hyssop plant and dip the brush in the bowl that has the blood of the animal in it. Then brush some of the blood above the door and on the posts at each side of the door of your house.

40

Faith in the Face of Fear

Sometimes the rain pounds down so hard and the winds howl with such intensity that it's deafening. Thunder roars with fury from above as lightning zigzags, streaking the sky with its powerful, unnerving presence. We are tossed about, battered from stem to stern, as we ride the waves of despair and dread—just trying to survive. With all the noise, we struggle to hear Christ in the midst of the storm.

> God is our refuge and strength,
> an ever-present help in trouble.
> Therefore we will not fear,
> though the earth give way
> and the mountains fall
> into the heart of the sea,
> though its waters roar and foam,
> and the mountains quake with their surging.
> Psalm 46:1-3

James used the metaphor of a storm at sea when he talked about trials. He warns we will all face storms and without faith we will be "like a wave of the sea, blown and tossed by the wind."[1] We cannot kid ourselves and pretend that if our faith is strong, we will never be afraid. We certainly will, but we don't need to live as slaves to fear, allowing it to control or change us. Fear can be managed with faith. When our faith is securely anchored in Christ, bold courage can rise from within as we step out in confidence, trusting Him to battle the object of our fear. The disciples had some room for growth in the courage department. One day when they were in a boat on the Sea of Galilee, their faith came unglued! Jesus was with them, peacefully asleep, when a sudden and intense storm swept over them. Terrified, they awakened Jesus for help. He asked them to choose between fear and faith. "Why are you so afraid? Do you still have no faith?"[2] Notice He uses fear and faith in the same passage, each opposing the other. Yielding to fear such that it controls and sometimes paralyzes us implies no faith.

Jesus asks us the same thing

When the report comes in, when tragedy hits, when the phone call brings news of disaster, keep your head up. Don't let panic overtake you. Fear is a terrible coping mechanism. Be still. Take deep breaths. Pray. Listen for the comforting voice of your Savior through the pelting scatter of wreckage showering down upon you. You don't face this disaster alone. God is in your crisis.

Jesus can calm any storm we face if we just stand on our faith. Do we want peace amidst our storms? It can only come from Jesus, the Prince of Peace.[3]

Satan's primary objective

We must know with confidence what we believe before the storms blow in. Satan's primary objective is to attack our faith. If not solidly anchored in Christ, it will waver in times of stress and fear. C.S. Lewis asserted, "Christianity, if false, is of no importance, and if true, is of infinite importance. The one thing it cannot be is moderately important."ᴬ

When faith is attacked, fear skyrockets. Fear is a dreadful enemy and thief; its venom robs us of hopes and dreams. We can face our storms with courage, but only if we place our trust in Jesus and allow Him to take charge and navigate our passage.

What fears are you facing? Is a storm surging out of control? Are the breakers of anxiety and emotions crashing over you, their waves pounding you mercilessly? Is the booming thunder of the roaring tide drowning out His voice? Jesus knows every storm you are facing and will face in the future. There is no reason to panic.

God has a purpose for your life—to solve some of the world's problems through you. This is no time to tremble and shrink back in fear. It's time to rise up in faith— shoulders back, head held high! You and God will work together to move mountains and part waters. Push fear aside and walk forward in bold, faith-filled confidence.

Two strategies for dealing with fear

Charles Spurgeon used two biblical examples to show how our faith interfaces with our fear.

- David states, "When I am afraid, I put my trust in you."[4]
  This is faith that helps us deal with fear.
- Isaiah states, "I will trust and not be afraid."[5]
  This is faith that keeps fear away.

Both approaches are biblical, but perhaps Isaiah had the better idea.

Your storm

No matter what your storm looks like or how it lashes out, you can call on God in the midst of it—at any time. He will calm the storm, although it may not be right away. Perhaps He wants to ride it out with you as you learn to lean on Him and trust Him even more. Regardless, He sets the boundaries and says, "This far and no further."

But consider calling on God *before* the storm because faith drives out fear before it can take root. Active faith brings glory to God and is visible to others who are watching.

As you refuse to succumb to fear and actively trust God to navigate your course through the crisis, you reflect His power in the presence of faith. How much faith do you need? The faith of a mustard seed—the smallest of all seeds.[6]

---

[1] James 1:6
[2] Mark 4:40
[3] Isaiah 9:6
[4] Psalm 56:3
[5] Isaiah 12:2b
[6] Matthew 17:20b – If you have faith as small as a mustard seed, you can say to this mountain, "Move from here to there," and it will move.

41

~⁓

Spiritual Blindness

There was a church in a wealthy city named Laodicea. It is the last of the seven churches addressed in Revelation. Located in modern-day Turkey, this church was likely planted by Epaphras, one of the apostle Paul's disciples. It was so large, it spanned an entire city block.[A] (This church was ultimately struck by a devastating earthquake in the 7th century A.D. and was subsequently abandoned.[A])

The city of Laodicea was once a major seaport. A thriving city, it boasted a state-of-the-art medical center where they manufactured a pill in tablet form; it was used to heal a wide range of eye diseases. The people crushed the tablet, mixed it with a little water, and applied it to their eyes. It became a famous eye salve that was exported to the surrounding areas.[B]

Despite being a prosperous and thriving city, Jesus disapproved of the prevailing immorality in Laodicea. He addressed the Laodiceans, using a metaphor they would readily understand. He called them blind[1]—spiritually blind. They needed more than their famous salve to see clearly! They needed the Truth of God. Jesus told them if they didn't follow God, they'd never see clearly; this would have eternal repercussions.

Your vision

What determines the way you see the world? In a sermon, Dr. David Jeremiah posed this question, "Do you view the world through the lenses given to you by the Holy Spirit and have you ground those lenses in the pages of the Holy Scripture? Or has the spirit of the age placed a set of lenses over your eyes you don't even realize is there?"[C]

This is a piercing question that should give us pause! Is it possible Satan has put lenses over our eyes, distorting reality—and we don't even know it?

Perhaps we've foolishly discarded God from our daily lives, opting instead to live our lives for ourselves, relying on our own wisdom and understanding. We have created our own false reality. This is a recipe for disaster!

> Trust in the LORD with all your heart
> and lean not on your own understanding;
> in all your ways submit to him,
> and he will make your paths straight.
> Proverbs 3:5-6

As imperfect beings, our understanding is distorted and perspective is limited, whereas God's understanding is limitless. The enemy blinds us and we can't tell what is truly happening. Best to rely on God and submit to His purposes, trusting Him—holding nothing back. We must saturate ourselves in God's Word and prayer, so we won't be led astray. It's the *only* way to cure spiritual blindness and walk with 20/20 vision into a life brimming with joy and a future full of hope and promises.

---

[1] Revelation 3:17b – You do not realize that you are wretched, pitiful, poor, blind, and naked.

42

~⁓~

Wisdom From Heaven

We can puff ourselves up all day long with knowledge of earthly things, as well as knowledge of the Bible, but we often miss the one ingredient that defines a wise person: fear of the Lord. This fear the Bible talks about doesn't mean terror or fright. Rather, it is a reverent awe of His holiness, majesty, and divinity—the realization that we cannot begin to grasp even a tiny portion of its magnitude.

When we embrace and express this fear, He ushers us through the doorway to holy wisdom—true and profound.

> The fear of the LORD is
> the beginning of wisdom.
> Proverbs 9:10a

A healthy fear of the Lord is the place out of which true wisdom flows—not the fake wisdom of the world.

The contemporary surge of information has seen explosive growth. Relentless newsbites bombard us rapidly and incessantly throughout the day. Search engines grant instant 24/7 access to any information we seek. We can visit websites, download books, listen to thousands of podcasts, and even take college courses online at Harvard and Yale. Tweets, notifications, memes, alerts, and updates blow up our phones continually.

Our minds, perpetually connected to streams of information, remain inundated with facts, data, reports, and alerts. The average person today processes about 74 GB of information per day, the same amount consumed 500 years ago by a highly educated person in a lifetime! And that number grows about 5% each year.[A] There has never been a time in history filled with greater access to information. But possessing knowledge and knowing how to apply it are not the same thing.

> "Knowledge is horizontal.
> Wisdom is vertical;
> it comes down from above."
> Billy Graham

Wisdom is realizing God is everything and we are not. He is the Creator; we are the creation. This realization comes from an appreciation of His holiness.

> The wisdom that comes from heaven
> is first of all pure; then peace-loving, considerate,
> submissive, full of mercy and good fruit,
> impartial and sincere.
> James 3:17

When we live with holy fear, we live a God-centered, obedience-focused, worship-filled life. It's the natural response to the profound magnitude of His love for us. His eye is upon us, His presence is with us, His power and protection are for us, and His love consumes us.[1] John tells us, "God is love."[2] Love is God's identity. Its vastness no one can comprehend.

Neither death nor life,
neither angels nor demons,
neither the present nor the future,
nor any powers, neither height nor depth,
nor anything else in all creation,
will be able to separate us from the love of God
that is in Christ Jesus our Lord.
Romans 8:38-39

No one is able to love to the extent God does. Mother Teresa contended, "Love, to be real, must cost. It must hurt. It must empty itself of self."

Though he was in the form of God,
[Jesus] did not count equality with God
a thing to be grasped, but emptied himself,
by taking the form of a servant,
being born in the likeness of men.
And being found in human form,
he humbled himself by becoming obedient
to the point of death, even death on a cross.
Philippians 2:6-8, ESV

Jesus's love for us cost Him dearly. When Someone loves us this much, we can trust Him. As believers, we should approach Him with a reverent fear, recognizing that everything God does is grounded in His immeasurable, sacrificial love for us.

For God so loved the world that he gave his
one and only Son, that whoever believes in him
shall not perish but have eternal life.
John 3:16

Our God is not to be feared as people of other faiths fear their gods. He is a God to embrace with praise, worship, obedience, service, and most of all, our love and trust. It's simple, yet profound. God's love reflects His glory.

> The fear of the LORD is pure,
> enduring forever.
> Psalm 19:9

Living in reverent fear of God reflects holy wisdom—true wisdom from above. It influences every aspect of our existence: from the way we live to the way we love. This transformative lifestyle doesn't go unnoticed; it leaves a profound and enduring impact.

May our love for others reflect our deep respect for God and His extravagant love, bringing hope to those who are suffering. May this truth saturate every corner of our being and fill us with incomprehensible joy.

---

[1] Ephesians 3:19a – To know this love that surpasses knowledge…
[2] 1 John 4:16b – God is love. Whoever lives in love lives in God, and God in them.

43

The Strength of Surrender

When you sense God calling you to do something beyond your abilities, how do you react? Do you immediately make a list of all the reasons you can't? If so, you're not telling God anything He doesn't already know; He knows all about your shortcomings. He's not seeking your input, nor your permission. Rather, He is calling you to trust Him and move forward in obedience.

Perhaps you compare yourself to other people and think they would be better suited for the task. You feel inferior. But get this—the task has nothing to do with your feelings or abilities. In fact, the task isn't about you at all.

God specifically designed you the way He did for a reason, and He needs you to be you. He didn't make a mistake in choosing you for what He has in mind. If you refuse God—the One who designed and created you— simply because you're afraid, you're telling Him you think you know more than He does. What an insult to our holy God! And you will miss the blessing of seeing what Christ can do in and through you. As you surrender to His will, God will equip you for whatever the task requires. You have all you need to successfully fulfill the mission He sets before you because you have Holy Spirit power.

Face it: no one can do *you* the way you can! Author John Roedel writes, "Your life is a song that will only be sung once."[A] Don't refuse to sing the song you are meant to sing or you will deprive the world of your unique gifts.

When you sense God calling you to do something beyond your perceived abilities, let the request drive you to your knees in humility and surrender. It's a huge honor and privilege to be chosen! Accept it with grace and gratitude.

Make no mistake—Satan will rear his ugly head and do all he can to make you feel insecure, inadequate, ill-equipped, and afraid. Ignore it all. Do not cave to these feelings. Instead, joyfully surrender to God's authority. William Booth, preacher and founder of the Salvation Army, said, "The greatness of a man's power is the measure of his surrender."[B]

Surrendering to God is an act of strength, not weakness. And the more we surrender, the stronger we become. When Paul acknowledged his weaknesses and insecurities before the Lord, he found this was when he was the strongest.[1] When we succeed through our weaknesses, we reflect God's power in our lives and He is glorified!

What is God calling you to do? Rise up. Author John A. Shedd wrote "A ship is safe in harbor, but that's not what ships are for."[C] A ship is built for one purpose: to set out to sea. It's worthless sitting still and unused in the harbor. The same is true for us. We were designed for one purpose: to set out in the world in pursuit of the Kingdom agenda. Sure, we can refuse to go and stay home where it is safe. But that's not what we were made for. We were made to venture outside our comfort zone and take risks for the gospel. A wasted life is wasted glory.

---

[1] 2 Corinthians 12:9-10 – My power is made perfect in weakness …I will boast…about my weaknesses, so that Christ's power may rest on me…For when I am weak, then I am strong.

44

~

They Feared God

idwives have been around a long time—over 4000 years![A] In the King James Version of the Bible, *midwife* occurs three times and *midwives* are mentioned six times. All nine references are found in the books of Genesis and Exodus. The English term *midwife* can be dissected into two parts. Mid means "together with" and wif means "women." The word, in its entirety, means a woman helping other women in childbirth.[B]

Shiphrah and Puah were two remarkable women in the Old Testament. They were Hebrew midwives who lived during the Israelites' slavery in Egypt, around 1450 BC. Four hundred years earlier, Joseph had been a highly trusted and very powerful man in Egypt, second only to Pharaoh. He brought his family to Egypt during a famine so he could provide for and protect them. They were safe as long as Joseph was alive. But after Joseph died, new kings came into power in Egypt who didn't know Joseph or respect his importance and authority.

Because the Israelites were having lots of babies and their population was rapidly growing, the new king felt threatened; he was afraid the baby boys would grow up and join enemy troops if a war broke out. Reacting in fear, he assigned slave masters to oppress them, requiring extremely brutal labor. But the oddest thing happened—the more they were abused, the more they multiplied. The slave masters doubled down, working them even harder. They were merciless, making the Israelites miserable. Yet, it didn't slow the rate at which they were multiplying.

With evil intent, the king of Egypt had another idea! He called Shiphrah and Puah into his presence. (It is likely there were many midwives; Shiphrah and Puah may have been their overseers.) The king gave them a chilling order. As they delivered the babies, they were to kill the baby boys, but allow the baby girls to live. The boys were a threat as they would grow up to be warriors.

If his plan succeeded, the pharaoh would have destroyed the next generation of Hebrew males. The Hebrew girls would have become their slaves or perhaps married off to Egyptians and become part of the Egyptian race. The Israelite nation would effectively be eliminated. Most importantly, if the Jewish race ceased to exist, there would be no promised Messiah.

God would not permit this to happen. He promised to make Abram's descendants into a great nation[1] and to bless the entire world through them—from whom Jesus the Messiah would come.[2] It's fascinating that God used two Jewish midwives to outwit Pharaoh and fulfill His greater plan.

And outwit him they did! Moses tells us twice that Shiphrah and Puah feared God[3]—obviously far more than they feared the pharaoh. So, they chose to obey God rather than the Egyptian king. They told Pharaoh that the Hebrew women gave birth before the midwives could arrive. The implication: they were powerless to carry out the murder of newborn Hebrew boys. Was this the truth or a lie? We don't know; it is possible the midwives purposely chose not to arrive until just after the babies were born.

This is the first act of civil disobedience cited in Scripture—choosing to obey God rather than a civil law that dishonors Him. When the laws of men conflict with the laws of God, Christians are to obey God, not men.[4] The midwives' faith emboldened them to stand for what they knew was right and they spared the lives of the Hebrew boys. (This is the first biblical instance where the issue of infanticide or full-term abortion is addressed.)

God was well pleased with the midwives for courageously risking their lives to prevent genocide and save the Hebrew nation. He honored them by granting children during a time when it was dangerous for Hebrews to have children.[5] Children are precious to the Lord, His most precious gifts. I would be curious to know if Shiphrah and Puah had sons (who would have been killed), daughters, or both.

> Children are a gift from the LORD,
> the fruit of the womb is a divine reward.
> Psalm 127:3, CEB

It is noteworthy that we are provided with the names of these two faithful servants of God, recorded for all history, yet we do not know the name of the king of Egypt. We know he was a pharaoh, but *pharaoh* simply means an ancient Egyptian king. The Bible doesn't tell us which pharaoh this specifically was.

Shiphrah and Puah give us much to consider. In Bible times, some regarded midwives as people of a lowly status, yet these midwives served to the best of their ability while making sure their actions glorified God. It was a noble calling indeed!

What tasks lie before you today? Perhaps some important undertakings. But maybe some lowly duties as well. Whatever we do today, we are called to regard our work as an act of service to God as well as to work in a way that gives Him glory.[6] When you see your duties as honoring the Lord, they take on special significance with eternal implications.

> Always give yourselves fully to the work of the Lord,
> because you know that your labor
> in the Lord is not in vain.
> 1 Corinthians 15:58

Always obey God's laws. Stand up for what is right. Treat people with respect and kindness. Work with integrity as you reflect Jesus to a lost and floundering world. As you reflect Jesus, He is glorified, and people notice! God will reward you mightily and generations that come after you will benefit from your faithfulness!

For His glory!

---

[1] Genesis 12:2-3 – I will make you into a great nation, and I will bless you; I will make your name great, and you will be a blessing. I will bless those who bless you, and whoever curses you I will curse; and all peoples on earth will be blessed through you.

[2] Acts 3:25b – He said to Abraham, "Through your offspring all peoples on earth will be blessed."

[3] Exodus 1:17, 21

[4] Acts 5:29 – Peter and the other apostles replied: "We must obey God rather than human beings!"

[5] Exodus 1:20-21 – God was kind to the midwives and the people increased and became even more numerous. And because the midwives feared God, he gave them families of their own.

[6] Colossians 3:23b – Whatever you do, work at it with all your heart, as working for the Lord, not for human masters.

45

~∾~

The Walking Dead

A man approached Jesus—but not just any man. He was covered with ugly sores, scaly skin, and deformed extremities. By law, he knew he was supposed to stay away from people, but he was desperate. This man had leprosy, a hideous, detestable, incurable disease—the most feared disease in the ancient world!

The symptoms

Leprosy initially broke out in painless, subtle red spots on the skin which gradually increased in size and number as the disease spread. The lesions became inflamed and ulcerated. The skin lost its color and became shiny, scaly, and thick. The skin around the eyes and ears bunched "with deep furrows between the swellings, so the face started to look like that of a lion."[A]

In that day, many people thought leprosy was a disease of the skin, but it is actually a disease of the nervous system.[B] The bacterium destroys the nerve endings[B] of the hands and feet, robbing the victims of feeling such that they are unable to detect pain. When lepers suffer injuries or burns, they often don't realize it because of the loss of sensation.[A] In Jesus's day, wounds became infected and gangrene quickly set in. As a result, fingers, toes, hands, feet, and ears eventually fell off.[C]

Some lepers had their fingers eaten by rats in their sleep![B] Disfigurement of the skin and bones occurred as limbs twisted and fingers curled into claws.[B] Skin became dry and peeled off in scales.[C]

Sometimes their eyes rotted away. The nose collapsed as bone was destroyed. The bacilli attacked the larynx, making their voices raspy. Hair fell out. Fingernails and toenails became loose and detached. Joints of fingers and toes rotted. Gums shrank until teeth eventually fell out. [A]

Due to leprosy, parts of their body would rot, emitting a foul odor that people could detect as they approached. [A]

Requirements of the law

Anyone suspected of having leprosy had to go to the priest for an examination. If leprosy was identified, the law required him to wear torn clothes, keep his hair unkempt, cover his mouth, live alone outside the city, and yell, "Unclean! Unclean" when approaching others.[1] "Among the 61 defilements of ancient Jewish laws, leprosy was second only to a dead body in seriousness."[D] Lepers weren't to come within six feet of any person, including family, and within 150 feet of anyone when the wind was blowing.[D] They were never to drink from a running stream where others might partake, nor sit on a roadside stone where another person might rest.[C]

Lepers were not allowed to enter the synagogue.[C] When diagnosed with leprosy, all relationships with other people ended; lepers were total outcasts. They were referred to as the living dead. Sometimes funerals were even held for them while they were still alive.[A]

A vivid depiction of sin

Charles Spurgeon compared leprosy to the debilitating impact of sin in our lives.

> "Every man by nature is like a leper...
> He is shut out utterly and entirely
> by his sin from the presence
> and acceptance of God."
> Charles H. Spurgeon

Like leprosy, sin starts off small; we barely notice. But sin goes deeper than the skin and it spreads. It is ugly, loathsome, alienating, and incurable. It defiles and isolates us. Like leprosy, sin affects the whole person.

The leper saw Jesus

One day, a leper living in the tombs saw Jesus from a distance. He ran toward Him and fell on his knees with his face to the ground, begging, "Lord, if you are willing, you can make me clean."[2] He was desperate! So desperate that he broke the law as he humbly approached Jesus, identifying Him as "Lord." He asked for healing.

Jesus was filled with compassion and "reached out his hand and touched the man,"[3] curing him of leprosy. Jesus, the friend of the outcast, had compassion and was willing to heal him. The Mosaic law forbade people to touch lepers and become unclean.[4] No one touched lepers.

Except Jesus.

How about us?

Until we, too, come to Jesus, we are the living, walking dead—dead in our sins. We must come before Jesus in humility (fully aware of our desperate condition), identify

Him as our Lord, and ask for mercy. He will not turn us away. Jesus became our sin and went to the cross so we could be whole.

> God made him who had no sin
> to be sin for us,
> so that in him we might become
> the righteousness of God.
> 2 Corinthians 5:21

A valuable gift

Pain, it turns out, is a valuable gift. It is a survival mechanism that warns us of danger. Without pain—without suffering—we might be like lepers, unable to discern when something is wrong or harmful. Dr. Paul Brand, a world-renowned hand surgeon and expert on leprosy, confided "I cannot think of a greater gift that I could give my leprosy patients than pain."[B]

Whether physical, emotional, or spiritual, let's not be too quick to eliminate all pain in our lives. It may be God's warning signal that something is seriously wrong, and we should go to Him in humility, seeking restoration.

Pastor John MacArthur observed, "Just as leprosy destroys physical health and makes a person an outcast with other men, so sin destroys spiritual health and makes a person an outcast with God."[E]

Christ removed this man's leprosy. He can also eliminate sin. Just as His cleansing from leprosy restored the man to human fellowship, His cleansing from sin restores us to divine fellowship with God.

Anyone who has never trusted Jesus is spiritually worse off than the leper was physically.

Obedience is vital

Jesus sent the leper away with a strong warning:

> "See that you don't tell this to anyone.
> But go, show yourself to the priest and
> offer the sacrifices that Moses
> commanded for your cleansing…"

Instead, he went out and began…spreading the news.

> As a result, Jesus could no longer
> enter a town openly
> but stayed outside in lonely places.
> Yet the people still came to him from everywhere.
> Mark 1:44-45

The priest offered the designated sacrifice[5] so the man could be declared clean and received back into society and the synagogue. The man, however, disobeyed Jesus and told everyone! The crowds flocked to Jesus, creating a serious problem, hindering His teaching.

How have we hindered Jesus because of our disobedience? Today Jesus commands the exact opposite: to tell everybody about Him—and we keep quiet!

Today

Leprosy can now be cured. According to the World Health Organization, as of November 2022, about 208,000 people worldwide are infected with leprosy; most live in Africa and Asia.[F] Between 150 and 200 people are diagnosed with leprosy in the U.S. every year,[G] mostly in Florida, California, Hawaii, Louisiana, New York, and Texas.[H] At the time of this writing, 80% of cases are in Florida.[G]

---

[1] Leviticus 13:45-46
[2] Luke 5:12b
[3] Mark 1:41-42
[4] Leviticus 5:3
[5] Leviticus 14:1-32

46

You Had One Job!

"You had one job! Just one."

And I blew it!

I was a young teenager. It was our parents' anniversary. My brother, Scott, and I had planned a small family celebration. I was responsible for the cake. We successfully sneaked it into the house and tucked it away in my bedroom. As I was carefully placing the candles on the cake, Mom knocked on the closed door. Panic gripped us! Scott and I quickly considered our limited options. In haste, I placed the cake on the carpet on the other side of my bed—a place not visible from the door.

I opened the door and nonchalantly answered Mom's question. I quickly closed the door and returned to the cake—wiping my brow in relief that I dodged a bullet. Only to discover that Jo-Jo, our standard poodle, was having a celebration of her own as she had begun to merrily devour one side of the cake! She was beyond elated!

I had *one* job! Just one.

When it comes right down to it...

All of us have only one job. We live our lives, thinking it will last such a long time. Yet the days quickly slip between our fingers, seemingly picking up speed with each passing year. If we don't intentionally focus on the present, we will be swept up into the whirlwind. If we aren't careful, we'll miss it—the *one* task we must complete before the end of our lives: determining where we will go when we die.

> Everyone must die once
> and then be judged.
> Hebrews 9:27, NCV

Our earthly lives here will one day come to an end; no one makes it out alive. We all know this, yet many of us live as if we will never die.

A university student once asked Billy Graham this question. "What is the greatest surprise you have found about life?" Without hesitation, he replied, "The brevity of it." In his autobiography, *Just as I Am*, he stated, "Time moves so quickly and no matter who we are…the time will come when our lives will be over."[A]

Nothing is more important

The Bible is clear; judgment is coming. We must take eternity seriously. In his book, *And the Angels Were Silent*, Max Lucado states,

> "Our task on Earth is singular—
> to choose our eternal home.
> You can afford many wrong choices in life…
> But there is one choice that must be made correctly
> and that is your eternal destiny."[B]

Think of the time we spend planning a vacation. We spend hours reading about various destinations. We scour the internet to find the best flights at the cheapest prices. We plan our activities and tours, outlining all the options.

We book our hotel, schedule time off from work, hold our mail, arrange for pet care, pay our bills, and pack our bags. Many of us spend far more time planning for our annual vacation than we do our final destination for eternity! Nothing is more important—as the repercussions will last forever, which is an exceptionally long time!

Every person will live forever. No one will ever stop living. We will take our last breath on this earth and our very next breath on the other side of this reality. We exhale here—then we inhale there. God allows us to choose where "there" is. It's called free will.

Two choices

When Christ returns, everyone will recognize Him and His almighty authority and power—not just Christians, but every—single—person. It will be unavoidable.

At the mere mention of the name of Jesus, every knee will bow, and every tongue will confess He is Lord.

> Every knee will bow down before Me.
> And every tongue will say
> that I am God.
> Isaiah 45:23b, NLV

We have a choice. We can either *choose to accept Jesus* as Lord of our lives now as a step of loving commitment OR we can *be forced to acknowledge Jesus* as Lord when He returns. Bowing before Him now means salvation. We will spend eternity with Him—in Paradise—forever. If we reject Jesus, He won't force Himself on us, but will allow us to have our way—spending eternity separated from Him and every good thing—forever.

Choose wisely! Jesus will honor the choice we made while alive on this earth. Waiting until we die, or He returns is too late. His return could be today or tomorrow. Are you prepared?

You have one job—just one!

47

Solar Eclipse

A solar eclipse—when the Sun, Moon, and Earth are precisely aligned so the Moon blocks the Sun. This results in a portion of Earth being engulfed in the shadow cast by the Moon. Have ever witnessed a solar eclipse in person? Bob and I drove to South Carolina on August 21, 2017 to see "The Great American Eclipse." The sky darkened from Oregon to South Carolina in the first total solar eclipse visible from coast to coast across the United States in 99 years!

All of North America was able to witness at least a partial solar eclipse. Since we were in the totality zone, we saw it most dramatically; it became dark at 2:38pm for about 2-1/2 minutes. Crickets began to chirp and as the sun reemerged, roosters began to crow. It's intriguing how every aspect of nature seems attuned to the light. The light before and after the eclipse was both unsettling and remarkably eerie. It is difficult to adequately describe.

The Bible tells of another time when it got dark during the day. It is described in three of the four gospel accounts as well as in the Roman archives. This was not an eclipse. At noon, darkness descended "over the whole land until three in the afternoon"[1] as Jesus was crucified. The Sun did not shine from noon until 3pm[2] when "Jesus breathed his last."[3]

The Light of the world

There are seven I AM statements in the Bible that refer to Jesus. Each one describes an aspect of His identity. In His second I AM statement, He said, "I am the light of the world."[4] When He died, the light went out; it was totally dark, but it wasn't forever. He would rise again.

I would like to suggest we all live in our own spiritual eclipse when the darkness of the world blocks out (or eclipses) the SON—our Savior. We can't see or hear Jesus at times; He seems so far away and silent.

Some days we live in the light and everything goes our way. But sometimes, it's as if the world has gone dark.

What eclipses or blocks out Jesus for you? Fear? Anxiety? Depression? Busyness? Comfort? Pleasure? What about temptations? Addictions? I would bet some of you struggle with alcohol, some with food or shopping. Perhaps with social media, video games, or gambling. Anything done in excess can be damaging and eclipse Jesus from our lives.

The world screams its counterfeit claims of truth while Jesus whispers His divine Truth. We must tune in so we can hear the only Truth that will set us free[5] from the junk that fills our lives and blocks Jesus from view. These distractions cause us to live in darkness and bondage, whether for a few hours or much longer.

A day of darkness is coming

The Bible tells us in the following verses that when Christ returns, God will cause the Sun to go down at noon and darken the earth in broad daylight.

The sun will be turned to darkness
and the moon to blood before the coming of
the great and dreadful day of the LORD.
Joel 2:31

———

The sun and moon will be darkened,
and the stars no longer shine.
The LORD will roar from Zion
and thunder from Jerusalem;
the earth and the heavens will tremble.
Joel 3:15-16a

———

"In that day," declares the Sovereign LORD,
"I will make the sun go down at noon
and darken the earth in broad daylight."
Amos 8:9

———

The stars of heaven and their constellations
will not show their light.
The rising sun will be darkened
and the moon will not give its light.
Isaiah 13:10

That day will be a day of darkness in which God will pour out His wrath upon the world. I expect it will feel far more eerie than what we felt during the solar eclipse we experienced.

Isaiah[6] and Revelation[7] tell us that in Heaven there will be no more night. No more darkness. But there will also be no more sunlight or moonlight because the Lord will be our eternal light. His presence will be the only light we will need.

Until that day, we live in this fallen and corrupt world of spiritual darkness. It is clouded by so much sin and evil that strive to eclipse the eternal light of Jesus in our lives.

We are called to fight against this darkness and evil. Stay plugged into the Source of divine light. Let nothing eclipse Jesus from your life. He's always there—guiding, leading, protecting, strengthening, comforting, and loving.

Our world is confused and lost, in desperate need of the light of Christ. Will you reflect His light and shine with joy and love for all the world to see? May His light expose and pierce the darkness and evil with its brilliance—the untouchable glory of God!

---

[1] Mark 15:33

[2] Mark 15:33

[3] Mark 15:37

[4] John 8:12

[5] John 8:32

[6] Isaiah 60:19 – The sun will no more be your light by day, nor will the brightness of the moon shine on you, for the LORD will be your everlasting light, and your God will be your glory.

[7] Revelation 22:5 – There will be no more night. They will not need the light of a lamp or the light of the sun, for the Lord God will give them light.

48

Whose Fires?

J don't know what your world looks like. Are you facing great challenges right now? Are troubles finding you at every turn? Are you heartbroken? How are you coping with many unknowns? Where are you turning? Consider this advice:

> You who live in your own light
> and warm yourselves
> from your own fires
> and not from God's;
> you will live among sorrows.
> Isaiah 50:11, TLB

When hardships come, the great prophet Isaiah warns us to have the courage to live amid the darkness of suffering, rather than lighting our own fire to seek a quick escape. This will only lead to sorrow. Instead, God has another way.

Scoot up one verse.

> If you are walking in darkness,
> without a ray of light,
> trust in the Lord
> and rely on your God.
> Isaiah 50:10b, NLT

We will not escape this life without being wounded by the darkness. Trusting God will bring a peaceful confidence as He navigates a way for us through our dense jungle of tangled and frightening challenges. He will guide our steps and, in His timing, lead us out of the darkness.

There will be times when the magnitude of our problems will seem overwhelming. We may feel helpless as we envision no way out. Don't panic, for God not only notices us struggling, but is also fully engaged. He sees the future and knows how this will play out for His imminent glory. He will provide the light we need at just the perfect time.

Isaiah urges us to relax. And to quit trying so hard to escape the darkness by lighting our own fires: calling friends, pooling resources, checking horoscopes, etc. Seeking our own light will only result in more sorrow. Author Lettie B. Cowman cautions,

> Do not try to get out of a dark place, except in God's time and in God's way. The time of trouble is meant to teach you lessons that you sorely need. Premature deliverance may frustrate God's work of grace in your life. Just commit the whole situation to Him. Be willing to abide in darkness so long as you have His presence.[A]

Wise words indeed, yet difficult to remember when sorrows lay siege. God invites us to seek the light from His fires and walk in the glimmer of those sparks. God is crafting a great work in our darkness. We must resist the temptation to interfere.

Stephen Merritt says it best:

> You touch anything of His, and you mar the work. You may move the hands of a clock…but you do not change the time; so you may hurry the unfolding of God's will, but you harm…the work. You can open a rosebud but you spoil the flower. Leave all to Him.[A]

As we grope in the darkness, let's remember He is always with us, guiding us, and protecting us:

> Whether you turn to the right or to the left,
> your ears will hear a voice behind you, saying,
> "This is the way; walk in it."
> Isaiah 30:21

We all encounter sorrows

When we are consumed with one dark day upon another, we can see His light most clearly as it takes only a flicker to catch our attention. John tells us, "The light shines in the darkness"[1] —a reminder that our ever-present God is our enduring hope and our greatest comfort. Therefore, we must lean into Him with every step as we slog through the hard times. And He blesses us in our suffering.

At times it seems so dark we cannot discern anything good. We see no beauty in our days. Yet the darkness around us exposes His light dwelling within us. Never question in the dark what God tells you in the light. Don't suppress that light. Thank God our darkness is temporary; it lasts for just a season. It is during our periods of darkness that we must move closer to Him, warm ourselves in His fire, and allow His truths to carry us. It is far better to abide with God in the darkness and seek the pure light of His divine fires than walk alone in the world's "light."

As we trust Him, He lovingly provides us with tender mercies and blessings to sustain us through the long days.

> I will give you the treasures of darkness
> and riches hidden in secret places,
> so that you may know that it is I, the Lord,
> the God of Israel, who call you by your name.
> Isaiah 45:3, NRSV

Let's walk confidently through life's darkness, relying upon God to bring us through. Let's seek moments of joy, reasons to smile, and opportunities to be thankful.

We may entertain thoughts of escaping our sorrows, but if we do, we miss the riches He has tucked within the depth of our struggles. As we endure, embracing our suffering in the strength of the Lord, His blessings will sustain us. And our faith will grow as we see His faithfulness.

Beauty from the suffering

One day we will behold the most exquisite masterpiece—the transformation that unfolded during our darkest days, as God shaped us into the image of Christ.

> "If God can bring blessing from
> the broken body of Jesus and glory from
> something that's as obscene as the cross,
> He can bring blessing from
> my problems and my pain
> and my unanswered prayers."
> Anne Graham Lotz

The darkness is no reason to fear. Let's push through in faith, abiding in and reflecting His glory, trusting unwaveringly in God's greater purpose. Suffering isn't meaningless. Our suffering leaves scars that God will transform into glory. He will bring beauty from our pain—joy from our tears—hope from our desperation. All in His perfect timing. In God's economy, nothing—absolutely nothing—is ever wasted.

This world is not our home; it is filled with trouble, but that's ok. It gives us an eternal perspective and makes us yearn for Heaven even more, which is coming soon, my friend. It's coming soon. In full glory.

Praise God!

---

[1] John 1:5a

49

～❦～

Be Encouraged

$\mathcal{L}$ ife is hard—just plain hard sometimes. We often suffer in silence; it's not easy to admit to others that life is ambushing us and we could use some encouragement. Sometimes we are quietly living our lives, only to be assaulted with challenges—without warning. Life was going well…until it wasn't. Life has suddenly been turned upside down. And we wonder, "What just happened?"

It is humbling to realize how many people we pass every day in our mundane daily lives who must be fighting some kind of battle and as such, are vulnerable. Some people are barely holding it together.

He is only 27 and has just been diagnosed with cancer. His dad is an abusive alcoholic. She is only 31 and her mother is in the final stages of early-onset Alzheimer's Disease; she loses a bit of her every day. They have only enough retirement savings to last another three months. He suffered severe brain damage at the age of 29 due to a nursing error. Their daughter, 16, ran away two weeks ago and they can't find her. All his earnings go to support his next hit and the addiction has him in a vice. He is elderly and lives alone; his children rarely call or show interest. She has rheumatoid arthritis and suffers daily pain in joints too numerous to count. Her son was diagnosed with neurosarcoma and died five months later, just after his 31st birthday. It's time to take the final step and downsize from the family home to a nursing home. She is young, pregnant, single, and scared. Perfectly healthy a year ago, he now suffers from a potentially fatal heart condition. Five friend couples lost a young adult son in the last six months.

All these scenarios are real.

Like you, they could use a word of encouragement. Pastor John Maxwell asserts, "Encouragement is oxygen for the soul." It's something we all need. Heartache is everywhere. Many people struggle and suffer in silence, yet as we go about our daily errands, we probably can't pick them out.

A perfect apple

I recently admired a seemingly perfect apple—a glistening, beautiful piece of fruit. But when I turned it around, I noticed a festering, rotten spot on the other side. The apple wasn't so perfect. Things aren't as they appear—social media is a perfect example. We never know the whole story as we peer into a small window of the lives of others. We all carry blemishes, yet we usually only show the world the unblemished side.

As a society, we have become masters of disguise. We get up in the morning, put on our mask, and go about our day, often with a smile on our face and a quick, "I'm fine" on our lips when asked, "How are you?"

Yet not all is fine. Could you use a word of encouragement today?

Put down that piece of carrot cake or the bowl of mint chip ice cream. Turn off the TV. Set aside your phone. Instagram can wait. Pick up your Bible instead. Look what treasure awaits:

For everything that was written in the past
was written to teach us,
so that through the endurance
taught in the Scriptures
and the **encouragement** they provide
we might have hope.
Romans 15:4 (emphasis mine)

Everything—not some things—not most things—not a thing or two, but *everything*—in Scripture provides encouragement to give us hope. That's quite a claim!

Even the challenging parts of the Bible are included to ultimately encourage us in some way. That's why it's so important to spend time in our Bible every day...time alone with God, talking to God, listening for answers, and seeking direction.

The more time we spend in God's Word, the more He lifts the heavy clouds of discouragement. God's Word is living and active.[1] It contains enormous power and offers true encouragement and hope.

You're my place of quiet retreat;
I wait for your Word to renew me.
Psalm 119:114, MSG

Could you use a word of encouragement today? Joshua reminds us not to be discouraged because God goes with us wherever we go.[2] There's nothing you can do to shake Him loose; He's stuck to you like glue!

Where can I go from your Spirit?
Where can I flee from your presence?
If I go up to the heavens, you are there;

if I make my bed in the depths, you are there.
If I rise on the wings of the dawn,
if I settle on the far side of the sea,
even there your hand will guide me,
your right hand will hold me fast.
Psalm 139:7-10

God is not only with you; He's speaking to you, cheering you on, encouraging you. He's offering you living hope.

Praise God that He sees all of us—the entire apple—and carries us through the challenges and loves us no matter what! Although we struggle and fail, through the blood of Christ we are seen as unblemished and whole for eternity. We look like Jesus! As others watch us, they see Him reflected in our words and actions—in the way we love others. This is worth celebrating!

Take heart. Be encouraged. God is on your side, even if no one else is. Even if no one fully understands your losses, the depth of your suffering, the ways you stumble, or the extent of your stress.

And that is enough.

---

[1] Hebrews 4:12a, ESV

[2] Joshua 1:9 – Be strong and courageous. Do not be afraid; do not be discouraged, for the LORD your God will be with you wherever you go.

50

I'm Too Bad

𝒥f you died today, are you confident you will go to Heaven? It's a question we all need to ask ourselves. I asked a young friend this very question. He became evasive. His answer wasn't brief. Here are some of the statements he made.

- "I'm too bad."
- "I have done some awful things."
- "Nobody knows the extent of what I've done."
- "It's too late for me."

There is one truth we need to know well: the things we've done do not determine our final destination. There's nothing you and I can do to earn our way into Heaven—no number of good deeds—no amount of begging or bargaining with God. Our ticket to Heaven has nothing to do with our works.[1] That's not God's way. Quite frankly, none of us deserve to be there. Christianity is the only religion that claims man cannot work his way into Heaven.

And no matter the number of awful things we have done, it's never enough to keep us out of Heaven. It's not too late. This is why Jesus came to Earth and died the death you and I deserve. He paid for our ticket when we couldn't buy it for ourselves. This is God's way.

Our sin nature is a problem—a big problem!

All have sinned and fall short
of the glory of God.
Romans 3:23

We are all born with a sin nature which separates us from God. Left unresolved, our sin will result in eternal separation from God. He set the rules ahead of time, then wrote them down for us in the Bible so nothing is a surprise, nor out of our control; we are free to choose our eternal path.

Many people think there are big sins and little sins, but they are wrong. There is just sin, and sin cannot be allowed into Heaven. Just as darkness cannot exist in the presence of light, sin cannot exist in the presence of a holy God. If sin entered Paradise, it would no longer be Paradise!

The Bible says there is only one way to get to Heaven. People will tell you all roads lead to Heaven, but there is only one; all other ways are dead ends. This may appear narrow-minded, intolerant, and exclusive, yet it's intentional according to God's design. Jesus made it very clear.

I am the way and the truth and the life.
No one comes to the Father except through me.
John 14:6

The way. Singular. Not one of many ways. Only one—through Jesus who came from Heaven to connect with us. His sinless life qualifies Him to redeem us from our sins.

In him is no sin.
1 John 3:5b

The great exchange of the gospel

Jesus willingly suffered and died to pay the price our sins demanded: death.

> For the wages of sin
> is death.
> Romans 6:23a

Jesus paid a debt He didn't owe because we owed a debt we couldn't pay. His death opened the way for us to enter Heaven and live forever with Him.

> God made him who had no sin
> to be sin for us,
> so that in him
> we might become
> the righteousness of God.
> 2 Corinthians 5:21

This is the great exchange of the gospel. Jesus takes our sin and shame upon Himself. In exchange, He gives us His perfect righteousness. When God sees us, He sees the righteousness of Jesus, NOT our sin.

As a result, God offers us salvation as a gift.

> The gift of God is eternal life
> in Christ Jesus our Lord.
> Romans 6:23b.

We must do one thing

We must accept this gift by confessing Jesus is Lord. Here are several verses that make this process crystal clear.

For God so loved the world
that he gave his one and only Son,
that whoever believes in him
shall not perish but have eternal life.
John 3:16

Believe in the Lord Jesus,
and you will be saved.
Acts 16:31

If you declare with your mouth, "Jesus is Lord,"
and believe in your heart
that God raised him from the dead,
you will be saved.
Romans 10:9

When we trust in Jesus as our personal Savior, we are promised eternal life in Heaven because our sins are forgiven—and forgotten! It sounds ridiculously simple—too simple. This is purposeful; a child can understand it!

I will be merciful to them in
their wrongdoings, and I will
remember their sins no more.
Hebrews 8:12, TLB

If Jesus has forgiven your sins and doesn't remember them anymore, it's okay for you to let them go. Let go of past failures. If you don't leave your past in the past, it will destroy your future. Satan tortures us with forgiven sins. Do NOT allow him to torment you any longer. He has no power over you—unless you give him that power. Why would you allow this evil enemy to have control over you?

Live for what today has to offer, not for what yesterday has stolen.

> If the Son sets you free,
> you will be free indeed.
> John 8:36

You are not at the mercy of your circumstances or your sinful inclinations. It doesn't matter how bad you've been or the awful things you've done. Totally irrelevant.

This is what's relevant: God's love for you has never changed. When judgment and self-condemnation threaten to knock you down, God will break your fall if you reach for Him—and allow Him to save you.

We are all sinners in desperate need of God's grace, and there's only one way we are saved—by believing in the death and resurrection of Christ. Will you accept the sacrifice of Jesus Christ for you? May you be able to grasp just how profoundly precious you are to Him.

Your eternal destination is up to you—it's called free will. God gives you a choice.

> "If you live for the next world,
> you get this one in the deal;
> but if you live only for this world,
> you lose them both."
> C.S. Lewis

If you want to choose this narrow way to Heaven and accept Jesus as your Lord and Savior, please pray this prayer out loud to reflect your faith in Jesus Christ and commit your life to Him.

"Lord Jesus, I know I am a sinner; every sin I commit is against You. Please forgive me. I believe You paid for my sins by taking the punishment I deserve. You died for my sins, then rose from the dead. I turn from my sins and the life I have been living. I invite You to come into my heart and my life. I place my trust in You for salvation. I want to trust and follow You as my Lord and Savior for the rest of my life. Thank You for the gift of eternal life in Heaven with You. Amen."

If you genuinely prayed this prayer, you will spend eternity with Jesus in Heaven. Tell someone. Find a church and start attending regularly. Buy a Bible and start reading it every day. Join a Sunday School class or a small group at church. Get baptized. And please reach out to let me know of your decision. What a blessing this would be to me. You can email me at: Kim@kimskinney.com

Congratulations! You have made a monumental decision today. Write down this date. You'll remember this moment always.

Today, on _____ I profess faith

(today's date)

in Jesus Christ.

_____

(your signature)

---

[1] Ephesians 2:8-9 – For it is by grace you have been saved, through faith—and this is not from yourselves, it is the gift of God— not by works, so that no one can boast.

Closing Prayer

Father God,

You have filled the world with glory—all of it reflecting you, its Creator. And You didn't stop there! You filled each one of us with Your glory in the form of the Holy Spirit. This is mind-boggling. The love You have for us is outrageous! We cannot begin to comprehend it! Show us how to embrace it and live in a way that we shine the light of Your glory and Your love, piercing the darkness of our world for eternity. Help us to walk worthy of Your holiness.

We praise You and we love You.

Amen

A Request

It has been my great privilege to share this second book in The Glory Series with you. I pray it blessed you.

Did it make you smile, laugh, cry, or think? (Bonus points if it did all four!) Please consider writing a short review on Amazon and Goodreads. Your reflection could be exactly what someone else needs to hear.

Simply scan the QR codes below to share your thoughts! This makes a big impact. Keep reflecting His glory. Thank you! ♥ Kim

You may use this QR code to post to Amazon.

Use this QR code to post to Goodreads.

I'd love to know your favorite chapter(s) and topic(s). Your comments will be very helpful as I continue to write. Please feel free to email me at Kim@kimskinney.com.

Notes

Introduction

   A. Piper, J. (2004). *Seeing and Savoring Jesus Christ.* (Rev. ed.). Wheaton, IL: Crossway.

The Glory of God Quote Page

   A. Quote by Anne Graham Lotz
Lotz, A. G. (2009). *Just give me Jesus.* (2nd ed.). Nashville, TN: Thomas Nelson, Inc. p. 155.

   B. Quote by Douglas McKelvey
McKelvey, D. K. (2017). *Every moment holy.* (Vol. 1). Nashville, TN: Rabbit Room Press. p. 206.

Chapter 1 – Reflecting His Glory

   A. Durham, M. (2016, June 7). *What is the glory of God?* Real Truth Matters. https://realtruthmatters.com/2016/06/07/what-is-the-glory-of-god/#.Y0B7W3bMK3A

   B. Piper, J. (2016). A peculiar glory: How the Christian *scriptures reveal their complete truthfulness.* Wheaton, IL: Crossway. p. 150.

   C. Stonestreet, J. & Morris S. (2022, December 19). Earth crammed with heaven: God's glorious works. *Breakpoint Daily: Colson Center.* https://www.breakpoint.org/earth-crammed-with-heaven-gods-glorious-works/

Chapter 2 – Boomerang Blessing

A. Barnett, A. (2023, September 8). *Sun.* NASA: Solar System Exploration. https://solarsystem.nasa.gov/solar-system/sun/overview/

B. *Sun.* (n.d.). StarDateOnline. https://www2.nau.edu/~gaud/bio301/content/sun/sun.htm#:~:text=Today%2C%20the%20Sun%20continues%20to,which%20makes%20the%20Sun%20shine.

C. Harvey, A. (2022, January 21). *How big is the sun?* Space.com. https://www.space.com/17001-how-big-is-the-sun-size-of-the-sun.html

D. Davis, P. (2020, February 1. Updated 2023, August 17). *How big is the solar system?* NASA: Solar System Exploration. https://solarsystem.nasa.gov/news/1164/how-big-is-the-solar-system/#:~:text=As%20noted%20earlier%2C%20Earth's%20average,That's%201%20AU.

E. Cain, F. (2013, April 15). *How long does it take sunlight to reach the Earth?* Phys.org. https://phys.org/news/2013-04-sunlight-earth.html#:~:text=Photons%20emitted%20from%20the%20surface,the%20Sun%20to%20the%20Earth.

F. Fernandez, R. (2002, February 16). *How close can we get to the sun? NASA has a good idea.* ScreenRant. https://screenrant.com/nasa-close-can-get-sun-how/#:~:text=An%20astronaut%20in%20his%20suit,humans%20can%20get%20really%20close.

G. Evans, T. (2017, July 20). *When we see God's glory.* [Video]. Tony Evans Sermons.

https://www.youtube.com/watch?v=8rTb2IfOzNg
&ab_channel=TonyEvans

Chapter 3 – Your Roots Matter

A. Williamson, S. (n.d.). *What kind of root system do you have?* John Maxwell Team. https://johnmaxwellteam.com/what-kind-of-root-system-do-you-have/

B. Grisham, M. (2018, July 10). *How deep are your roots?* MollyGrisham. https://www.mollygrisham.com/blog/2018/7/10/hoe-deep-are-your-roots

C. *About coast redwoods.* (n.d.). California Department of Parks and Recreation. https://www.parks.ca.gov/?page_id=22257

D. Stanley, C. (2009, August 29-30). The influence of faith. *In Touch Ministries Daily Devotional.* https://www.crosswalk.com/devotionals/in-touch/in-touch-aug-29-30-2009-11606668.html

Chapter 5 – The Cockeyed Squid

A. *How far does light travel in the ocean?* (2020, December 4). National Ocean Service: National Oceanic and Atmospheric Administration. https://oceanservice.noaa.gov/facts/light_travel.html

B. *The curious eyes of the cockeyed squid.* (2017, February 13). Monterey Bay Aquarium Research Institute. https://www.mbari.org/the-curious-eyes-of-the-cockeyed-squid/

C. Hoover, A. (2017, February 13). *How this cockeyed squid shines a light on deep sea evolution.* The Christian Science Monitor.

https://www.csmonitor.com/Science/2017/0213/H
ow-this-cockeyed-squid-shines-a-light-on-deep-sea-
evolution#:~:text=The%20cockeyed%20squid%20
Histioteuthis%20heteropsis,for%20spotting%20biol
uminescent%20flashes%20below

Photo Credits

aa. *Histioteuthis.* (2006). National Oceanic &
Atmospheric Administration. Wikipedia Commons.
Public Domain.

bb. *Cockeyed Squid (Histioteuthis pacifica)* by SJADES.
(2018, March 27). Java, Indonesia.

Chapter 6 - Never Say Never

A. *What is the significance of the rooster crowing in regards to
Peter denying Jesus three times?* (n.d.). Got Questions
Ministries. https://www.gotquestions.org/rooster-
crowing-ssPeter.html

B. Carnegie, D. (2010). *How to stop worrying and start living.*
(Rev. ed.). New York, NY: Simon & Shuster.
https://www.whatyouwilllearn.com/book/how-to-
stop-worrying-and-start-living/

Chapter 7 – Free Fall

A. *What is the average skydiving height?* (2021, July 2).
Wisconsin Skydiving Center.
https://wisconsinskydivingcenter.com/blog/what-
is-the-average-skydiving-height/

B. *What will skydiving physically feel like?* (2019, April 30).
Skydive Snohomish.
https://www.skydivesnohomish.com/blog/what-
does-skydiving-feel-like/

Chapter 8 – Sheep in Human Clothing

A. *Shepherding our flock: Sheep have problems.* (n.d.). Above Rubies. https://aboverubies.org/index.php/2013-11-12-17-55-51/english-language/shepherding-our-flock/2485-shepherding-our-flock-sheep-have-problems

B. Challies, T. (2013, August 26). *Dumb, directionless, defenseless.* Challies. https://www.challies.com/christian-living/dumb-directionless-defenseless/

C. *Can sheep swim?* (n.d.). RaisingSheep.net. https://www.raisingsheep.net/can-sheep-swim#:~:text=Circumstances%20in%20Which%20Drowning%20is%20a%20Danger&text=The%20water%20makes%20the%20sheep's,to%20traverse%20is%20too%20large.

D. Piper, J. (2023, May 22). *Jesus knows his sheep.* Desiring God. https://www.desiringgod.org/articles/jesus-knows-his-sheep

E. Wilcox, G. (2018). *3 insights from the holy land to deepen your understanding of Christ's title as the "good shepherd."* LDS Living. https://www.ldsliving.com/3-insights-from-the-holy-land-to-deepen-your-understanding-of-christs-title-as-the-good-shepherd/s/89785

F. *I am the gate for the sheep.* (n.d.). Christ Church. https://christchurchtraversecity.com/sermons/i-am-i-am-the-gate-for-the-sheep-john-101-10/

G. Lynn, S. (2011, June 23). *The shepherd's oil.* Equip Her. https://equipherlife.com/2011/06/23/the-shepherds-oil/

H. Junquera, P. (2021, July 12). Nasal bot flies of sheep: biology, prevention, and control. In *Parasitipedia.*

https://parasitipedia.net/index.php?option=com_co
ntent&view=article&id=2554&Itemid=2832

I. Keller, W.P. (2007). *A shepherd looks at Psalm 23.*
Grand Rapids, MI: Zondervan. pp. 106-107.

J. Woodard, G. (2021, May 26). *6 ways sheep are like
people: Overcoming the grind of uncertainty.* Koinonia.
https://medium.com/koinonia/6-ways-sheep-are-
like-people-d126bd34a2b

K. Amelinckx, A. (2017, December 22). *6 fun facts about
sheep you might not know.* Modern Farmer.
https://modernfarmer.com/2017/12/6-facts-sheep-
might-not-know/

L. *Sheep senses.* (2021, April 19). Sheep101.info.
http://www.sheep101.info/senses.html#:~:text=Th
ey%20have%20excellent%20peripheral%20vision,in
%20front%20of%20their%20noses

Photo Credits

aa. *Flock of sheep on a watering hole.* © [Steftach]/Adobe
Stock. File #170456367.

bb. *Shepherd and flock.* © [Noel Powell]/Adobe Stock.
File #3341312.

cc. *Sheep in mountain. French Alps at Granges de Joigny.*
© [jefwod]/Adobe Stock. File #493192951.

Chapter 9 – A Blessing from Heaven

A. *Why is the grass wet in the morning?* (n.d.). Wonderopolis.
https://www.wonderopolis.org/wonder/why-is-the-
grass-wet-in-the-morning

B. *The blessing of dew.* (n.d.). One for Israel.
https://www.oneforisrael.org/bible-based-teaching-
from-israel/the-blessing-of-dew/

C. Cowman, L. B. (2023, January 30). *Refreshing dew.* Streams in the Desert. https://www.crosswalk.com/devotionals/desert/streams-in-the-desert-january-30th.html

Chapter 10 – Light Amid Darkness

A. Spurgeon, C. Updated and expanded by Reimann, J. (2008), *Morning by morning: The devotions of Charles Spurgeon.* Grand Rapids, MI: Zondervan. Day 94.
B. Evans, A. (2020, April 19). *The cure* [video file]. https://www.youtube.com/watch?v=4kcz5MCEAyo&ab_channel=TonyEvans
C. Rothschild, J. (2018, October 31). *Sister, you and I shine for Jesus! But did you know that our lights make us targets? When we shine...* Facebook. https://www.facebook.com/jennifer.j.rothschild/photos/sister-you-and-i-shine-for-jesus-but-did-you-know-that-our-lights-make-us-target/10156984574884994/

Chapter 12 – The Miracle Mile

A. *The miracle mile—1954—A Moment in Time.* (n.d.). http://www.miraclemile1954.com/
B. Tarbotton, D. (2017, August 7). *On this day—August 7—Vancouver miracle mile.* Commonwealth Games Australia. https://commonwealthgames.com.au/on-this-day-august-7-vancouver-miracle-mile/
C. Piper, J. (2023). *Don't waste your life* (3rd .. Wheaton, IL: Crossway.
D. *The sub-4 alphabetic register (1755 athletes as at 6 June 2022).* (2022, June 30). National Union of Track Statisticians.

http://www.nuts.org.uk/sub-4/Sub-4%20register%206%20June%202022.pdf

E. Mile run. (2023, August 17). In *Wikipedia*. https://en.wikipedia.org/w/index.php?title=Mile_run&oldid=1170802988

F. *Why bad runners (and leaders) look back at the finish line.* (2023, May 16). Prod101.com. https://prod101.com/why-bad-runners-and-leaders-look-back-at-the-finish-line/#close

G. Ray, M. (n.d.). Roger Bannister. *Britannica.* https://www.britannica.com/biography/Roger-Bannister

H. Brady, E. (2023, May 5, updated 2023, June 19). King Charles will make history, but he won't top Roger Bannister. *The Buffalo News.* https://buffalonews.com/news/local/history/erik-brady-king-charles-will-make-history-but-he-wont-top-roger-bannister/article_d60ad622-eb41-11ed-8b19-030f0f6347c0.html#:~:text=Bannister%20died%20in%202018.,year%20before%20Bannister's%20magical%20mile.

I. Obituary: Roger Bannister. (2018, March 4). *BBC News.* https://www.bbc.com/news/uk-11764114

J. *John Landy: Biography.* (n.d.). IMDb. https://www.imdb.com/name/nm1219458/bio/

K. Passa, D. (2022, February 26). John Landy, pursuer of Bannister's 4-minute mile, dies at 91. *Associated Press.* https://www.klfy.com/sports/national-sports/john-landy-pursuer-of-bannisters-4-minute-mile-dies-at-91/

Chapter 13 – Standing in the Gap

A. The NIV Life Application Bible: New International Version. (1991). Wheaton, IL: Tyndale House Publishers, Inc. & Grand Rapids, MI: Zondervan Publishing House. p. 132.

B. Evans, A. [@drtonyevans]. (2023, July 24). *When you pray, you usher in spiritual solutions to the problems at hand.* [Tweet]. Twitter. https://twitter.com/drtonyevans/status/168354610 0832108546

Chapter 14 – A Sacred Passage

A. Devine, M. (2017). *It's ok that you're not ok: Meeting grief and loss in a culture that doesn't understand.* Boulder, CO: Sounds True.

B. Lewis, C. S. (1961). *A grief observed.* New York, NY: The Seabury Press, Inc. NY, p. 62.

C. Leder, S. (2017). *More beautiful than before.* Hay House, Inc. Carlsbad, CA: Hay House, Inc., p. 6.

D. Lewis, C. S. (1961). *A grief observed.* New York, NY: The Seabury Press, Inc. NY, p. 69.

E. Lewis, C. S. (1961). *A grief observed.* New York, NY: The Seabury Press, Inc. NY, p. 68.

F. Langman, N. [@nicole_langman_officialprofile]. (2022, August 27).

G. Jimenez, G. (2022, January 12). Grief is like a pair of muddy boots. *The Hospice Heart.* https://www.thehospiceheart.net/blog/search/mud dy

H. Jimenez, G. (n.d.). *The Hospice Heart.* www.thehospiceheart.net

I.   McKelvey, D.K. (2017) *Every moment holy: New liturgies for daily life.* Nashville, TN: Rabbit Room Press. pp. 215-216.

Chapter 15 – Healing the Heart

A.   Vivian Green. (n.d.). [LinkedIn page]. (LinkedIn). https://www.linkedin.com/in/vivian-greene-1b37605/

B.   Keller, T. (2016). *Hidden Christmas: The surprising truth behind the birth of Christ.* New York, NY: Penguin Books. pp.93-94.

C.   Foust, M. (2023, May 19). *Tim Keller dies at age 72: 'I'm ready to see Jesus,' he said in final hours.* Christian Headlines. https://www.christianheadlines.com/contributors/michael-foust/tim-keller-dies-at-age-72-im-ready-to-see-jesus-he-said-in-final-hours.html

D.   Keller, T. (2016). *Making sense of God: An invitation to the skeptical.* New York, NY: Viking. p. 166.

E.   Hodges, S. & Leonard, K. (2011). *Grieving with hope: Finding comfort as you journey through loss.* Grand Rapids, MI: Baker Books. p. 54.

F.   Lamott, A. (2005). *Plan B: Further thoughts on faith.* New York, NY: Riverhead Books. p. 174.

Chapter 16 – Finding Calm Amid Chaos

A.   *Jesus boat found in Sea of Galilee near Magdala.* (n.d.). Magdalene Publishing. http://www.magdalenepublishing.org/uncategorized/discovery-of-the-jesus-boat-near-magdala/

B.   Caldwell, A. (2019, January 4). *The "Jesus Boat," an archeological treasure from the Sea of Galilee.*

https://aleteia.org/2019/01/04/the-jesus-boat-an-archeological-treasure-from-the-sea-of-galilee/

C. *Jesus boat*. (2022). See the Holy Land. https://www.seetheholyland.net/jesus-boat/

D. *The Jesus boat*. (n.d.). Early Church History. https://earlychurchhistory.org/commerce/the-jesus-boat/

E. Seismo. (2023). *Merriam-Webster.com*. https://www.merriam-webster.com/dictionary/seismo-

F. Rummage, S. Senior Pastor at Quail Springs Baptist Church in Oklahoma City, Oklahoma.

Photo Credits

aa. Trabantos. (2018, September 15). *An ancient wooden boat found in Ginsar, Israel*. [Photograph]. Shutterstock. Photo ID: 1323766310. https://www.shutterstock.com/image-photo/ginosar-israel-september-15-2018-ancient-1323766310

Chapter 17 – Surviving the Desert

A. Graham, B. (2018). *Just as I am: The autobiography of Billy Graham*. New York, NY: HarperCollins Publishers. p. 739.

Chapter 18 – Rivets of Steel

A. Ewers, J. (2008, September 25). The secret of how the Titanic sank. *U.S. News and World Report*. https://www.usnews.com/news/national/articles/2008/09/25/the-secret-of-how-the-titanic-sunk

B. Silen, A. (n.d.). Remembering the Titanic: Read about the tragic shipwreck in the frigid North Atlantic Ocean. *National Geographic Kids*. https://kids.nationalgeographic.com/history/article/a-titanic-anniversary

C. *RMS Titanic facts* (n.d.). Royal Museums Greenwich. https://www.rmg.co.uk/stories/topics/rms-titanic-facts

D. *NIST reveals how tiny rivets doomed a Titanic vessel.* (n.d.). National Institute of Standards and Technology. https://www.nist.gov/nist-time-capsule/nist-beneath-waves/nist-reveals-how-tiny-rivets-doomed-titanic-vessel#:~:text=This%20finding%20strongly%20suggested%20that,between%20the%20separated%20hull%20plates

E. Apr 15, 1912 CE: Titanic sinks. (n.d.). *National Geographic*. https://education.nationalgeographic.org/resource/titanic-sinks/

F. Lipman, D. (2012, April 11). The weather during the Titanic disaster: Looking back 100 years. *The Washington Post*. *https://www.washingtonpost.com/blogs/capital-weather-gang/post/the-weather-during-the-titanic-disaster-looking-back-100-years/2012/04/11/gIQAAv6SAT_blog.html*

G. *Titanic fast facts.* (2022, March 28). CNN Editorial Research. https://www.cnn.com/2013/09/30/us/titanic-fast-facts/index.html

H. *The iceberg that sank Titanic.* (n.d.). National Museum of American History.

I. https://americanhistory.si.edu/collections/search/o
bject/nmah_1416178#:~:text=Titanic%20struck%2
0a%20North%20Atlantic,of%20the%20adjacent%20
watertight%20compartments

J. Harish, A. (2023, May 22). *Why did the Titanic sink?
An engineer's analysis.* SimScale.
https://www.simscale.com/blog/why-did-titanic-
sink-engineer/

K. Guzman, F. (2023, June 20). Where is the Titanic
wreck located? Here's where Titan submersible
debris was found. *USA Today.*
https://www.usatoday.com/story/news/nation/202
3/06/20/titanic-wreck-location-map-missing-
submarine/70337395007/

Chapter 20 – Our Plumb Line

A. *Integrity.* (2014, June 20). The Berean's Desk.
https://bereansdesk.blogspot.com/2014/06/integrit
y.html?m=0

B. Lewis, C.S. *Mere christianity.* (1952). New York, NY:
Macmillan Publishing Company. p. 165.

C. Kyokwijuka, A. (2021, January 29). One of the truest
tests of integrity is its blunt refusal to be
compromised. *Monitor.*
https://www.monitor.co.ug/OpEd/Commentary/-
tests-integrity-compromised-schools-body-
language/689364-4254796- u55lycz/index.html#
:~:text=As%20one%20of%20the%20Africa's,deman
ds%20of%20the%20wrong%20side

Chapter 21 – Get Up!

A. Rivers, F. (2004). *The priest: Sons of encouragement.*
Wheaton, IL: Tyndale House Publishers. p 191.

Chapter 25 – Where is Your Battleground?

A. Original source unknown.

Chapter 26 – The Peace of Jesus

A. Dobson, E. (2012). *Seeing through the fog: Hope when your world falls apart.* Colorado Springs, CO: David C. Cook. p. 110.
B. Ibid, p.110.
C. Ibid, pp. 139-140.

Chapter 27 – Living Water

A. *Broken cisterns.* (2020, May 13). Savor Scripture. https://www.savorscripture.com/blog/broken-cisterns/
B. Morgan, M. (2023). *Cisterns in Bible times.* Bible Tales. https://www.bibletales.online/cisterns-in-bible-times/

Chapter 28 – A Risk Worth Taking

A. Graham, B. (1964, July). A Time for Moral Courage. *Readers Digest.* https://news.google.com/newspapers?nid=757&dat=19641029&id=rIcwAAAAIBAJ&sjid=lEQDAAAAIBAJ&pg=6379,1764784

Chapter 29 – Mysteries of the Gates

A. *How long was the journey from Babylon to Jerusalem?* (n.d.). ESV.org. https://www.esv.org/resources/esv-global-study-bible/facts-ezra-7/
B. *The gates of Jerusalem in Nehemiah's day.* (1994, February/March). Israel My Glory.

https://israelmyglory.org/article/the-gates-of-jerusalem-in-nehemiahs-day/

C. Gordon, I. (n.d.). *The meaning of the gates of Jerusalem: Gates of spiritual progression.* Jesus Plus Nothing. https://jesusplusnothing.com/series/post/nehem3

D. *Hezekiah's tunnel.* (n.d.). Biblical Archaeology Truth. http://www.biblicalarchaeologytruth.com/hezekiahs-tunnel.html

E. *Jerusalem's golden gate.* (n.d.). Magdalene Publishing. http://www.magdalenepublishing.org/blog/jerusalems-golden-gate-history-prophecy/

F. *What the Bible says about Miphkad.* (n.d.). Bible Tools. https://www.bibletools.org/index.cfm/fuseaction/Topical.show/RTD/cgg/ID/22680/Miphkad.htm

Photo Credits

aa. www.jesusplusnothing.com, used with permission.

bb. *The gate to old Jerusalem* by Castor, D. (2014, July 8). Public Domain.

cc. Meunierd. (2016, October 23). *The Muslim cemetery of Bab Al-Rahma adjoins the eastern wall of the Old City.* [Photograph]. Shutterstock. Photo ID 701443024. https://www.shutterstock.com/image-photo/jerusalem-israel-23-10-16-muslim-701443024

dd. My personal photo.

Chapter 30 – The Sacred Invades the Secular

A. Chambers, O. (1924). *My Utmost for His Highest.* Oxford, England: self published by his widow after his death.

B. Shirer, P. (2015). *Fervent: A woman's battle plan to serious, specific, and strategic prayer.* Nashville, TN: B & H Publishing Group.

Chapter 33 – Loving Porcupine People

A. Willis, D. & Willis, A. (2013). *Marriage minute: Quick and simple ways to build a divorce-proof relationship.* BookBaby Self-Publishing Company.

Chapter 34 – Slaves to Sin

A. *Isaac: with Abraham, twins and trials: Genesis 25-26.* [Class handout]. (2021). Bible Study Fellowship Lesson 16 Notes. p. 6.

B. *Video game addiction.* (n.d.). Addiction Center. https://www.addictioncenter.com/drugs/video-game-addiction/#:~:text=Moreover%2C%20video%20games%20affect%20the,video%20games%20may%20be%20possible.

C. Buffet, M & Clark, D. (2006). *The tao of Warren Buffett: Warren Buffett's words of wisdom: Quotations and interpretations to help guide you to billionaire wealth and enlightened business management.* New York, NY: Scribner. p. 16.

D. Bonhoeffer, D. (1954). *Life together: The classic and exploration of Christian community.* New York, NY: Harper & Row Publishers, Inc.

Chapter 35 – Breaking the Chains of Sin

A. Piper, J. (2004). *When I don't desire God; How to fight for joy.* Wheaton, IL: Crossway.

B. Chambers, O. (2023, June 23). *Acquainted with grief.* My Utmost for His highest. https://utmost.org/acquainted-with-grief/

C. *The return.* (2023). Life.Church. https://www.bible.com/reading-plans/21169-the-return/day/1

Chapter 36 – Their Finest Hour

A. Van Maren, J. (2017, August 1). *The real story of the "Miracle of Dunkirk."* The Bridgehead. https://thebridgehead.ca/2017/08/01/the-real-story-of-the-miracle-of-dunkirk/

B. Churchill, W. (1940, June 4). *We shall fight on the beaches.* [Speech transcript]. International Churchill Society. https://winstonchurchill.org/resources/speeches/1940-the-finest-hour/we-shall-fight-on-the-beaches/

C. Hong, P. (2017, August 12). *'But if not': How biblical literacy jolted civilian Brits into action at Dunkirk.* The Stream. https://stream.org/but-if-not-biblical-literacy/#:~:text=The%20message%20jolted%20the%20British,stalled%20and%20history%20was%20made.

D. Lambert, D. (1994, September 15). 'But if not." *Truth Magazine.* https://www.truthmagazine.com/archives/volume38/GOT038247.html

E. *Operation dynamo: The "Miracle of Dunkirk."* (n.d.). Beaches of Normandy Tours. https://www.beachesofnormandy.com/articles/The_Miracle_of_Dunkirk?id=36b15cff88

F. Stetzer, E. (2017). The epidemic of Bible illiteracy in our churches: How small groups can change the statistics. *Christianity Today.*

https://www.christianitytoday.com/pastors/2017/bible-engagement/epidemic-of-bible-illiteracy-in-our-churches.html

G. Dawes, Z. (2022, May 2). *'Unprecedented drop' in Bible engagement among U.S. adults.* GodFaithMedia. https://goodfaithmedia.org/unprecedented-drop-in-bible-engagement-among-u-s-adults/#:~:text=While%2077%25%20of%20U.S.%20adults,Bible%20Users%20since%20last%20year.

H. Religion news: 85 percent of U.S. households own a Bible. (2012, April 19). *Holland Sentinel.* https://www.hollandsentinel.com/story/news/2012/04/19/religion-news-85-percent-u/47661548007/

I. Braddy, K. (2017, July 10). *Discipling in an age of biblical illiteracy.* Lifeway Research. https://research.lifeway.com/2017/07/10/discipling-in-an-age-of-biblical-illiteracy/

J. Colson, C. (2017, August 7). Dunkirk, "And if not": The story behind the story. *Christian Headlines.* https://www.christianheadlines.com/columnists/breakpoint/dunkirk-and-if-not-the-story-behind-the-story.html

K. Churchill, W. (1940, June 18). *Their finest hour* [Speech transcript]. International Churchill Society. https://winstonchurchill.org/resources/speeches/1940-the-finest-hour/their-finest-hour/

Chapter 37 – From Complaining to Gratitude

A. *Defining and understanding the meaning of mercy.* (n.d.). Compassion International. https://www.compassion.com/poverty/mercy-definition.htm#:~:text=The%20word%20%E2%80%9Cmcrcy%E2%80%9D%20derives%20from,the%20sick%20or%20the%20poor.

Chapter 40 – Faith in the Face of Fear

A. Lewis, C. S. (2014). *God in the Dock.* New York, NY: HarperOne.

Chapter 41 – Spiritual Blindness

A. Sauter, M. (2023, February 16). *The church of Laodicea in the Bible and archaeology.* Biblical Archaeology Society. https://www.biblicalarchaeology.org/daily/biblical-sites-places/biblical-archaeology-sites/church-of-laodicea-in-the-bible-and-archaeology/

B. Myers, J. (2014, April 30). *Spittin' mad: The church at Laodicea.* Full Circle Refuge. http://www.fullcirclerefuge.org/2014/04/spittin-mad-part-1-of-2/

C Jeremiah, D. (2023, April 20). *The Prescription for spiritual blindness.* Prophecy Academy. [video file]. Prophecy Academy. https://www.lightsource.com/ministry/prophecy-academy-with-dr-david-jeremiah/the-prescription-for-spiritual-blindness-751055.html?ref=sc

Chapter 42 – Wisdom from Heaven

A. Heim, S. & Keil, A. (2017, June 1). *Too much information, too little time: How the brain separates important from unimportant things in our fast-paced media world.* Frontiers for Young Minds. https://kids.frontiersin.org/articles/10.3389/frym.2017.00023

Chapter 43 – The Strength of Surrender

A. Roedel. (2023, August 8). *I used to carry this note in my pockets wherever I went as a warning to quit comparing myself to…* Facebook. https://www.facebook.com/photo.php?fbid=10167559210765276&set=a.10150195026140276&type=3&eid=ARC-cbJM7rW2vBOjX2NIleIehIH_drcLwFh8p64x--jKwIfAX0u1Ftz31gOmJP9JKoxL5PegJ8K5ZkIL&paipv=0&eav=Afbs83O8zg-hKEJKP9VyQ4JymMjCkiAJtQ0ptJ-ZdJ0X-k0cX0eddzticuD6rA0COIo&_rdr

B. Warner, W. E. (1972). *1000 Stores and quotations of famous people.* Ada, MI: Baker Book House.

C. Shedd, J. A. (1928) *Salt from my attic.* Portland ME: Mosher Press.

Chapter 44– They Feared God

A. Overton, L. G. & Overton, B. (2001). *Midwifery and the Bible part I: Genesis 35:16-18.* Corpus Christi Birth Center. https://www.ccbirthcenter.com/midwifery-bible-i/

B. Midwife. (2016). *American Heritage Dictionary of the English language* (5th ed.). Boston, MA: Houghton Mifflin Harcourt Publishing Company. https://ahdictionary.com/word/search.html?q=midwife

Chapter 45 – The Walking Dead

A. LaPierre, S. (2023, March 27). *The ten lepers and their spiritual leprosy.* Scott LaPierre. https://www.scottlapierre.org/the-ten-lepers-and-spiritual-leprosy/

B. Gillen, A. L. (2009, October 25). *Biblical leprosy: Shedding light on the disease that shuns.* Answers in Genesis. https://answersingenesis.org/biology/disease/biblical-leprosy-shedding-light-on-the-disease-that-shuns/

C. Spurgeon, C. H. (1860, December 30). *The cleansing of the leper: A sermon delivered on Sabbath morning, December 30, 1860 by the Rev. C. H. Spurgeon at Exeter Hall, Strand.* The Spurgeon Center for Biblical Preaching at Midwestern Seminary. https://www.spurgeon.org/resource-library/sermons/the-cleansing-of-the-leper/#flipbook/

D. *Why is leprosy talked about so much in the Bible?* (n.d.). Got Questions Ministries. https://www.gotquestions.org/Bible-leprosy.html

E. MacArthur, J. (1987). *MacArthur New Testament commentary: Matthew 8-15 (Vol. 2).* Chicago, IL: Moody Press.

F.   Miller, K. (2022, November 12). *Leprosy (Hansen's Disease)*. WebMD. https://www.webmd.com/skin-problems-and-treatments/leprosy-symptoms-treatments-history#:~:text=Leprosy%20primarily%20affects%20your%20skin,after%20several%20weeks%20or%20months

G.   Peralta, E. (2023, August 6). *What's behind the increase in leprosy cases in Florida*. NPR. https://www.npr.org/2023/08/06/1192388382/whats-behind-the-increase-in-leprosy-cases-in-florida

H.   Grant, T. (2023, August 1). Cases of leprosy on the rise in Florida, report says. *ABC News*. https://abcnews.go.com/Health/cases-leprosy-florida-rise-cdc/story?id=101876654#:~:text=Most%20of%20the%20cases%20from,travelers%20coming%20to%20the%20U.S.

Chapter 46 – You Had One Job

A.   Graham, B. (1997). *Just as I am: The autobiography of Billy Graham*. San Francisco, CA: Harper Collins. p. 720.

B.   Lucado, M. (1992). *And the angels were silent: The final week of Jesus*. Portland, OR: Multnomah Press. p. 137.

Chapter 48 – Whose Fires?

A.   Cowman, L. B. (2023, March 30). *Walking in the light of your own fire*. Streams in the Desert. https://www.crosswalk.com/devotionals/desert/streams-in-the-desert-march-30th.html

Topical Index

(Organized by chapter title number, not page number)

Meet the Author

*K*im S. Kinney was born in Yankton, SD and lived a short while in Winner, a small rural town in the middle of the state. She and her brother, Scott, were raised mostly in Glendale, WI.

Kim has been involved with ministry her whole life. She has taught Bible to many ages from kindergarten through college age. Most recently her passion has been creatively teaching God's Word to young adults and women of all ages.

In 2005, she launched and led an international online ministry, The Edge, for young adults and professionals. During these years, the Lord birthed in her the desire to write.

She and her husband, Bob, make their home in Kannapolis, NC. They have two grown children. Justin lives in Knoxville, TN and is an award-winning author of suspense thrillers. Rebecca lives in Winston-Salem, NC and pours her writing talents into medical research papers. Both children are heavily involved with ministry.

Kim is active in church, the community, and with an international anti-human trafficking ministry. She enjoys time with her family and dogs, writing, reading, cycling, swimming—always seeking some fun adventure, which has gotten her into trouble from time to time. She says this only makes the adventure that much sweeter!

Let's Connect

Website: kimskinney.com

Email: Kim@kimskinney.com

Facebook | Instagram | Threads: @Kimskinneyauthor

LinkedIn: @Kimskinney

Amazon author page: amazon.com/author/kimskinney

Free Gift

When you sign up for emails on my website, you will receive a free gift: 42 inspirational, digital quote cards in color from The Glory Series. Below is a sampling of the cards you will receive. **kimskinney.com**